Limnological and Water-Quality Data from Wonder Lake, Chilchukabena Lake, and Lake Minchumina, Denali National Park and Preserve and Surrounding Area, Alaska, June 2006–August 2008

By D.A. Long and C.D. Arp

Prepared in cooperation with the National Park Service

Open-File Report 2010–1322

U.S. Department of the Interior
U.S. Geological Survey

U.S. Department of the Interior
KEN SALAZAR, Secretary

U.S. Geological Survey
Marcia K. McNutt, Director

U.S. Geological Survey, Reston, Virginia: 2011

For more information on the USGS—the Federal source for science about the Earth, its natural and living resources, natural hazards, and the environment, visit http://www.usgs.gov or call 1-888-ASK-USGS

For an overview of USGS information products, including maps, imagery, and publications, visit http://www.usgs.gov/pubprod

To order this and other USGS information products, visit http://store.usgs.gov

Contents

Figures

Tables

Conversion Factors and Datums

SI to Inch/Pound

Multiply	By	To obtain
Length		
centimeter (cm)	0.3937	inch (in.)
meter (m)	3.281	foot (ft)
kilometer (km)	0.6214	mile (mi)
micrometer (μm)	3.937×10^{-5}	inch
millimeter (mm)	0.03937	inch (in.)
nanometer (nm)	3.937×10^{-8}	inch
Area		
square kilometer (km^2)	3.861×10^{-1}	square mile (mi^2)
Volume		
cubic meter (m^3)	35.31	cubic foot (ft^3)
microliter (μL)	3.382×10^{-5}	ounce, fluid
milliliter (mL)	3.382×10^{-2}	ounce, fluid
liter (L)	2.642×10^{-1}	gallon (gal)
Flow rate		
meter per second (m/s)	3.281	foot per second (ft/s)
cubic meter per second (m^3/s)	35.31	cubic foot per second (ft^3/s)
Mass		
nanogram (ng)	3.527×10^{-11}	ounce, avoirdupois (oz)
microgram (μg)	3.527×10^{-8}	ounce, avoirdupois (oz)
milligram (mg)	3.527×10^{-5}	ounce, avoirdupois (oz)
kilograms per hectare per year [(kg/ha)/yr]	0.8921	pounds per acre per year [(lb/acre)/yr]

Temperature in degrees Celsius (°C) may be converted to degrees Fahrenheit (°F) as follows:

$$°F = (1.8 \times °C) + 32.$$

Datums

Vertical coordinate information is referenced to National Geodetic Vertical Datum of 1929 (NGVD 29).

Horizontal coordinate information is referenced to the North American Datum of 1983 (NAD 83)

Limnological and Water-Quality Data from Wonder Lake, Chilchukabena Lake, and Lake Minchumina, Denali National Park and Preserve and Surrounding Area, Alaska, June 2006–August 2008

By D.A. Long and C.D. Arp

Abstract

Growing visitor traffic and resource use, as well as natural and anthropogenic land and climatic changes, can place increasing stress on lake ecosystems in Denali National Park and Preserve. Baseline data required to substantiate impact assessment in this sub-arctic region is sparse to non-existent. The U.S. Geological Survey, in cooperation with the National Park Service, conducted a water-quality assessment of several large lakes in and around the Park from June 2006 to August 2008. Discrete water-quality samples, lake profiles of pH, specific conductivity, dissolved-oxygen concentration, water temperature, turbidity, and continuous-record temperature profile data were collected from Wonder Lake, Chilchukabena Lake, and Lake Minchumina. In addition, zooplankton, snow chemistry data, fecal coliform, and inflow/outflow water-quality samples also were collected from Wonder Lake.

Introduction

Each year, Denali National Park and Preserve (Denali) (fig. 1) attracts thousands of tourists, many of whom visit or camp at Wonder Lake and hike into the backcountry. This growing visitor pressure can impact lake ecosystems and their watersheds, due to waste disposal, habitat degradation, and drainage alterations. Global-scale atmospheric transport and deposition of trace metals or changes in precipitation chemistry also may affect Wonder Lake and other lakes in the sub-arctic interior on a larger scale. Additionally, global- or regional-scale climatic changes may fundamentally alter lacustrine systems. Yet only sparse data exist to develop a required baseline characterization of limnological and water-quality parameters to substantiate anthropogenic or climatological changes that may be occurring.

Previous data collections primarily were constrained to Wonder Lake, and included dissolved oxygen, temperature, and nutrient profiles (LaPerriere and Casper, 1976), bathymetric mapping (LaPerriere and Casper, 1976; Werner, 1990), bottom stratigraphy (Werner, 1990), and lake core analyses related to tephras (Child, 1995). The Western Airborne Contaminants Assessment Project (WACAP) collected water-quality samples from Wonder Lake, and analyzed lake cores and fish tissues for semi-volatile organic compounds (SVOCs) and heavy metals (Landers and others, 2008).

Purpose and Scope

This report contains limnologic and water-quality data collected by the U.S. Geological Survey (USGS) from June 2006 to August 2008 at five lake and two stream sites in the northwestern part of Denali National Park and Preserve and surrounding areas (fig. 2 and table 1). Because some of the data presently cannot be stored in the USGS National Water Information System (NWIS), this report provides a single source to disseminate data that might not otherwise be available to the public.

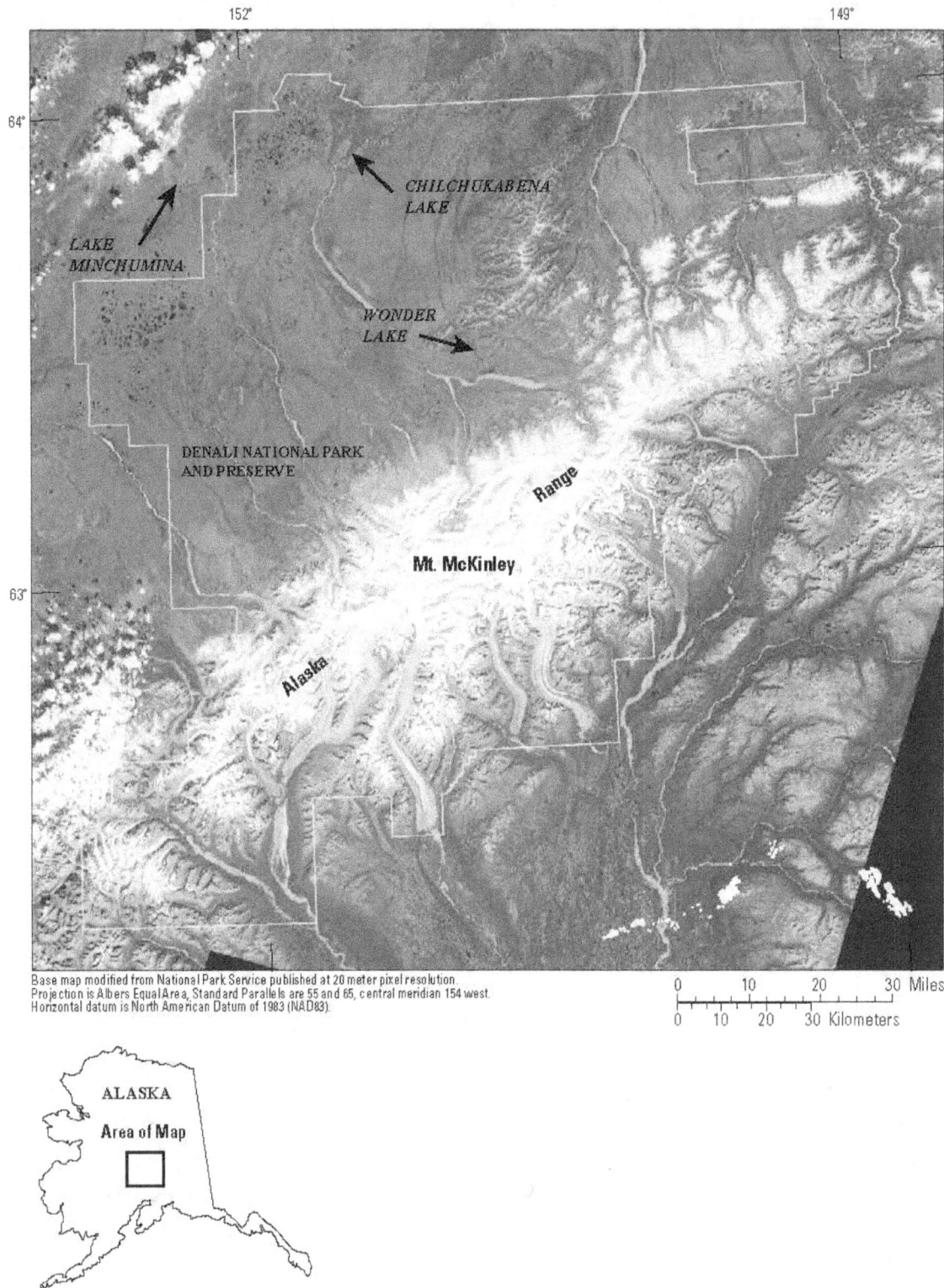

Figure 1.   Location of Wonder Lake, Chilchukabena Lake, and Lake Minchumina, Denali National Park and Preserve and surrounding area, Alaska.

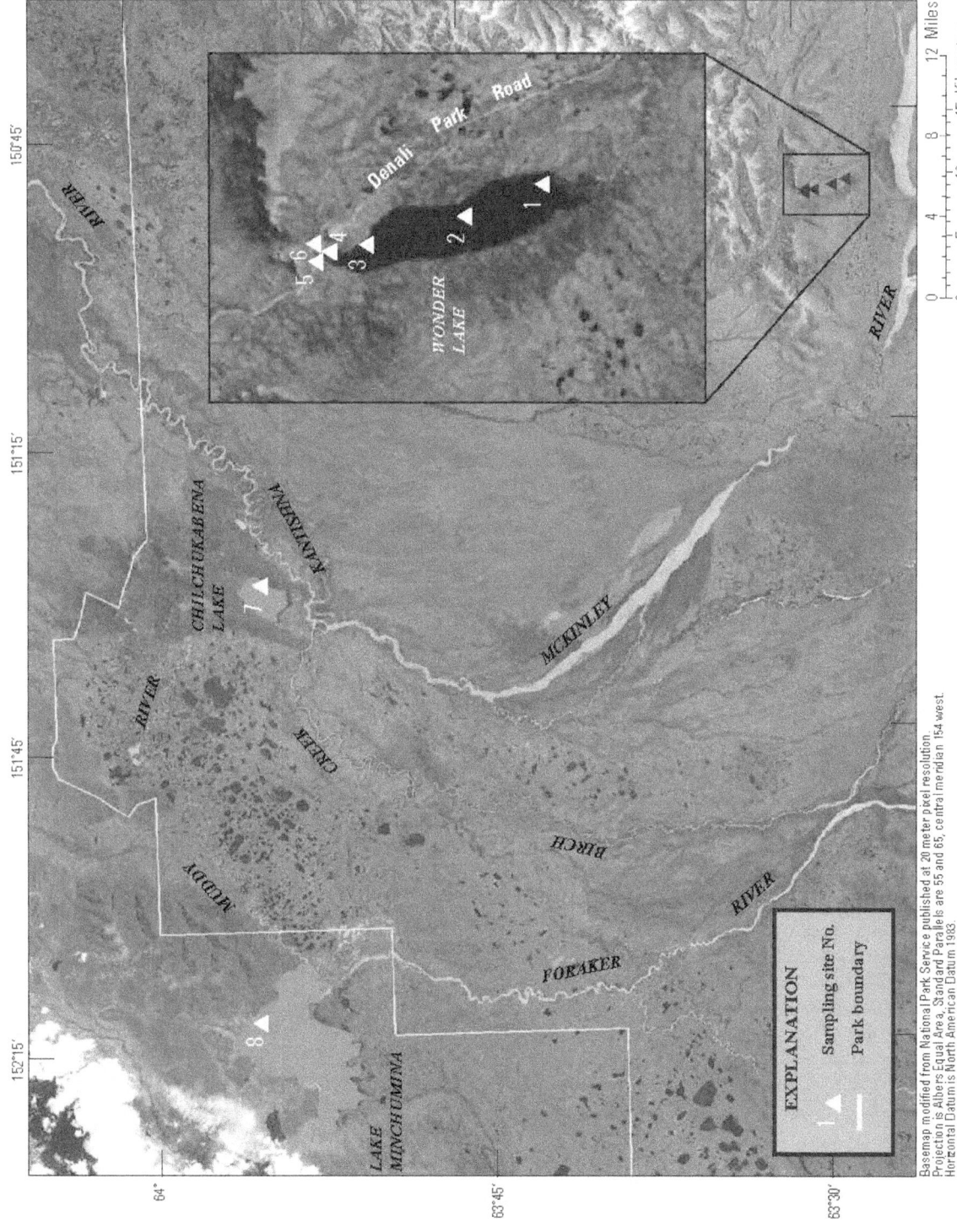

Figure 2.   Locations of data-collection sites at Wonder Lake, Chilchukabena Lake, and Lake Minchumina, Denali National Park and Preserve and surrounding area, Alaska.

Basemap modified from National Park Service published at 20 meter pixel resolution.
Projection is Albers Equal Area, Standard Parallels are 55 and 65, central meridian 154 west.
Horizontal Datum is North American Datum 1983.

EXPLANATION

1 △ Sampling site No.

— Park boundary

Table 1.   Description of data-collection sites and basin characteristics, Denali National Park and Preserve and surrounding area, Alaska.

[Location of sampling sites are shown in figure 2. Abbreviations: km², square kilometers; °, degrees; ', minutes; ", seconds; NAD 83, North American Datum of 1983; NGVD 29, National Geodetic Vertical Datum of 1929]

Sampling site No.	Site name	USGS Site No.	Latitude (NAD 83)	Longitude (NAD 83)	Drainage area (km²)	Elevation (meters above NGVD 29)
1	Wonder Lake Site 1 near south end near Denali National Park	632755150520200	63°27'53"	150°52'10"	34.4	610
2	Wonder Lake Site 2 near center near Denali National Park	632833150523100	63°28'31"	150°52'39"	34.4	610
3	Wonder Lake Site 3 near north end near Denali National Park	632921150525600	63°29'19"	150°53'04"	34.4	610
4	Wonder Lake Site 4 near inlet near Denali National Park	632937150525600	63°29'35"	150°53'04"	34.4	610
5	Lake Creek at Lake outlet near Denali National Park	632944150532000	63°29'44"	150°53'20"	34.7	610
6	Wonder Lake Tributary at Park Road near Denali National Park	632945150530100	63°29'45"	150°53'01"	20.4	610
7	Chilchukabena Lake Site 1 near Lake Minchumina	635452151291200	63°54'50"	151°29'20"	33.9	191
8	Lake Minchumina near Lake Minchumina	635526152120700	63°55'24"	152°12'15"	3,030	196

Description of Study Area

Denali National Park and Preserve is more than 24,000 km² in size and spans the central Alaska Range in interior Alaska, including North America's tallest mountain, Mount McKinley (locally known as Denali). The transition from the Alaska Range to the northwestern lowlands presents a pronounced elevation-driven environmental gradient, with active glaciers to the south dissolving northward into glacial outwash and relic dune fields and thence expanding into unglaciated, permafrost-rich regions with abundant thermokarst, fluvial lakes, and ponds. Wonder Lake is considered to represent the middle to upper elevations, and Lake Chilchukabena and Minchumina Lake represent the lower elevations of this gradient (fig. 1). The mechanisms of basin formation and current source waters for these lakes likely represent distinct end-members for large subarctic lakes, thus providing the context in which these lakes were selected for data collection.

Wonder Lake is 44 km north of Mount McKinley and is a clearwater lake covering about 2.6 km² in surface area and occupying a narrow (4.4 km long, 0.8 km wide), sharply inclined, moraine-dammed glacial trough. Bathymetric mapping indicates the presence of two primary basins separated by a prominent transverse ridge (fig. 3) (Werner, 1990). By surface area, it is the seventh largest lake in the park, yet at more than 70 m deep, it is likely the largest lake by volume. The drainage area encompasses about 34.4 km² (fig. 4). Three water-quality sampling sites (sites 1-3, fig. 2) were situated longitudinally from south to north to capture possible chemistry changes between basins. A single tributary stream meandering through beaver-dammed peatland areas to the east enters the northern end of Wonder Lake through a culvert under Denali Park Road (site 6, fig. 2), accounting for about 60 percent of the drainage area. Lake Creek, a high gradient, boulder rich, outflow stream draining Wonder Lake to the north (site 5, fig. 2), exits less than 100 m from the inflow stream, probably limiting circulation in the lake, and providing an explanation for the basin's low sedimentation rate (Werner, 1990).

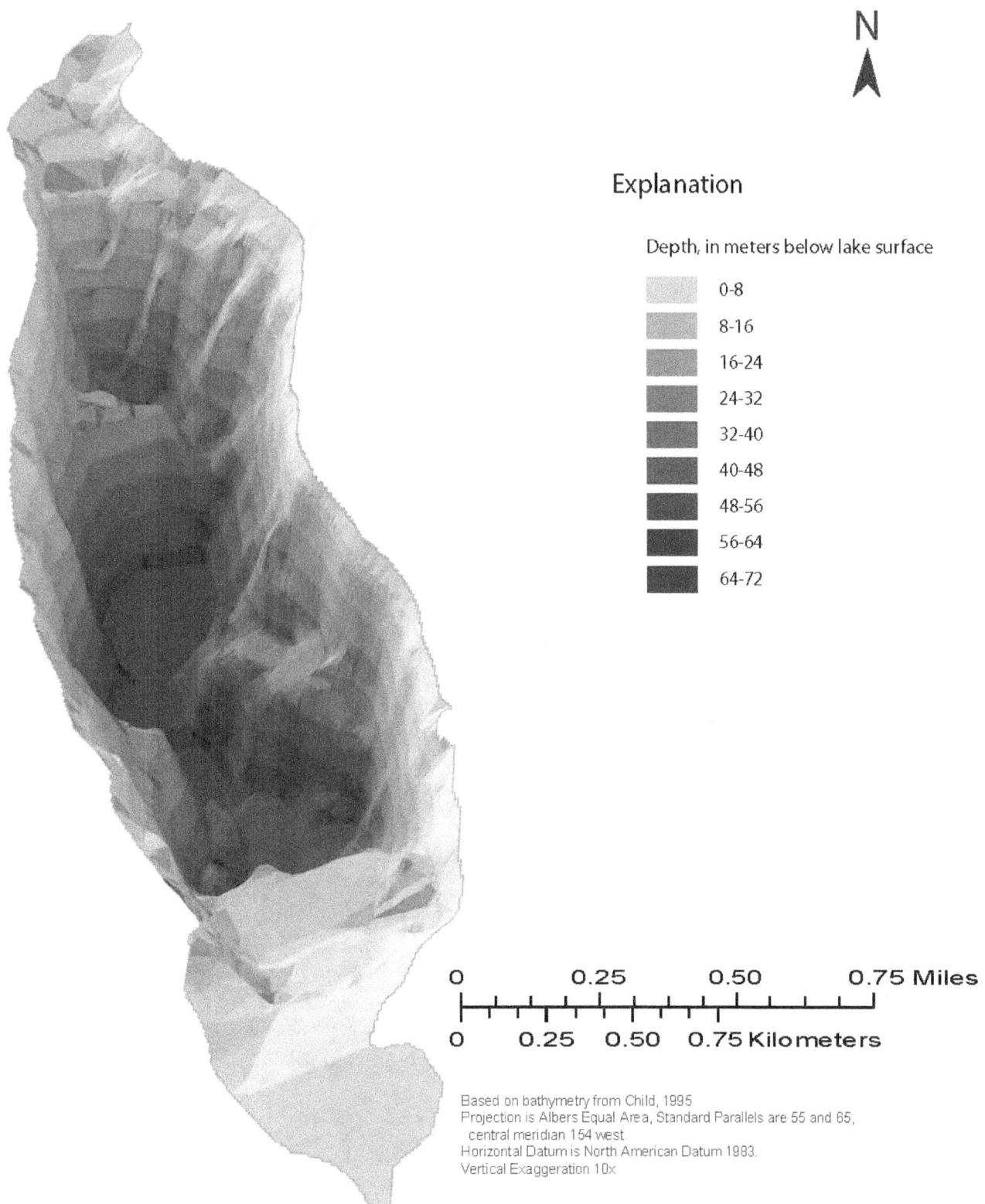

N

Explanation

Depth, in meters below lake surface

	0-8
	8-16
	16-24
	24-32
	32-40
	40-48
	48-56
	56-64
	64-72

| 0 | 0.25 | 0.50 | 0.75 Miles |

| 0 | 0.25 | 0.50 | 0.75 Kilometers |

Based on bathymetry from Child, 1995
Projection is Albers Equal Area, Standard Parallels are 55 and 65,
  central meridian 154 west.
Horizontal Datum is North American Datum 1983.
Vertical Exaggeration 10x

Figure 3.   Wonder Lake, Denali National Park and Preserve, Alaska.

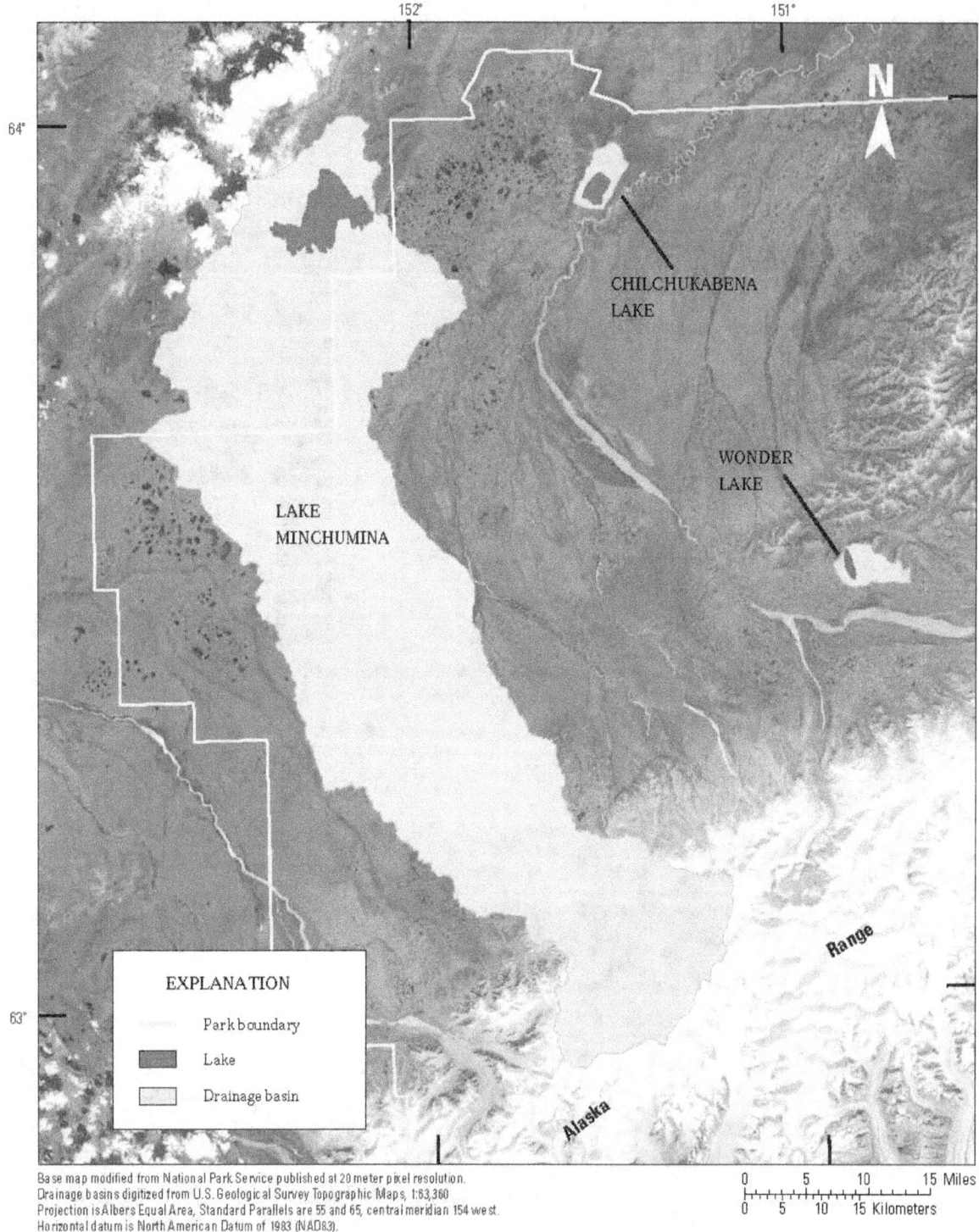

Base map modified from National Park Service published at 20 meter pixel resolution.
Drainage basins digitized from U.S. Geological Survey Topographic Maps, 1:63,360
Projection is Albers Equal Area, Standard Parallels are 55 and 65, central meridian 154 west.
Horizontal datum is North American Datum of 1983 (NAD83).

Figure 4.   Drainage basins of Wonder Lake, Chilchukabena Lake, and Lake Minchumina in Denali National Park and Preserve and surrounding areas, Alaska.

Chilchukabena Lake (site 7, fig. 2) near the northwestern corner of Denali is situated just north of the confluence of Birch Creek and the Muddy and McKinley Rivers. A surface area of 8.3 km² makes it the largest lake in the park; however, at less than 3 m deep, it is the shallowest of the lakes studied. Heavy vegetation growth and a soft organic-rich bottom support thick algal blooms and various aquatic avian fauna. The drainage area of about 33.9 km² (fig. 4) is similar to that of Wonder Lake, yet primarily originates from a single, south-facing slope. Chilchukabena Lake has no well-defined inflow or outflow channels, and the basin genesis is unclear.

Lake Minchumina (site 8, fig. 2) lies immediately outside the park boundary and appears to be the largest kettle lake in the area, covering 65 km² in surface area, although only attaining 12 m at its deepest point. In 2008, an estimated population of 17 inhabited the community of Lake Minchumina at the southwestern corner of the lake and various cabins distributed around the shoreline (Alaska Division of Community and Regional Affairs, 2010). The drainage area (3,030 km²), by far the largest of the three lakes, primarily lies within the park boundary, extending to the Alaska Range divide (fig. 4). Unlike Wonder or Chilchukabena Lakes, Lake Minchumina receives a heavy sediment influx from its primary inlet, the glacier-fed Foraker River, which enters at the eastern end. The silt plume produced by the Foraker River (easily observed from the air) indicates mixing to nearly the far western end of the lake. Annual runoff from the Foraker River is estimated to be 10 times the flow of the next smallest inlet (Kodama and others, 1983). The Muddy River is the single outlet of Lake Minchumina and exits from the eastern end of the lake proximal to the primary inlet. The water-quality sample site was placed near the northern shore in the silt-rich section of the lake.

Limnological and Water-Quality Data

The following sections describe sample collection techniques and analytical methods used at all sampling sites. A summary of site characteristics (latitude, longitude, drainage area, and elevation) is provided in table 1. Water-quality and lake profile data discussed in this section also are available from the USGS NWIS database (http://waterdata.usgs.gov/ak/nwis/).

Water-Quality Samples and Lake Profiles

Water-quality samples were collected in June, July, and September 2006 from Wonder Lake (sites 1-3). Ice-cover water-quality samples were collected in April 2007 from Wonder Lake site 3 and from Lake Minchumina. In June

2007, water-quality samples were collected from Wonder Lake (sites 2 and 3) and outflow and inflow streams (sites 5 and 6). Final samples were collected in August 2007 from all three lakes (site 2 only for Wonder Lake). In total, three sites were sampled at Wonder Lake along its length, one site was sampled at Chilchukabena Lake, and one site was sampled at Lake Minchumina.

A broad range of constituents were measured, including major ions, dissolved trace elements, nutrients, and biological indicators (chlorophyll-*a* and zooplankton at lake sites only). Additional sampling specific to Wonder Lake included a fecal coliforms assessment (*E-coli* and Enterococci, July 2006) and a single snow sample (collected April 2006) provided to WACAP for airborne contaminant analysis of semivolatile organic compounds (SVOCs) and metals (Landers and others, 2008).

Water-quality collection and processing procedures followed USGS National Field Manual (NFM) protocols (U.S. Geological Survey, variously dated). A two-person minimum field team collected samples to reduce the opportunity for contamination of low-concentration analytes, following the protocols of Horowitz and others (1994). Sampling and processing equipment was cleaned prior to each field trip following USGS NFM procedures. Equipment used for multiple sampling during a single trip was field rinsed numerous times with native water prior to reuse.

Lake water-quality samples were collected using a 6.2-L acrylic Van Dorn sampler. Depth profiles were collected prior to water-quality sampling for each lake sample site using a multi-parameter sonde to record field parameters (turbidity, dissolved-oxygen concentration, pH, specific conductance, water temperature, and uncorrected chlorophyll). Parameters generally were recorded at depth intervals of 1-m from water surface to lakebed, except at Wonder Lake site 2 where the recording depth interval was increased below the metalimnion to as much as 5 m. Lake-profile data for each fixed station are presented in table 8 (at back of report). For locations at Wonder Lake, near-surface (1–2 m depth) and near-bottom (1–3 m above lakebed) water-quality samples were collected and processed separately during each visit. Samples collected through ice, or from Chilchukabena Lake and Lake Minchumina (due to shallow depths), consisted of a single near-surface sample. Bacteria samples were collected as below-surface dip samples in sterile flasks. Alkalinity was obtained by incremental endpoint titration on a filtered, chilled sample, ordinarily within 8 hours of sample collection.

Streamflow sampling followed USGS National Field Manual techniques for nonisokinetic dip samples due to minimal discharge (0.03–0.06 m³/s) and sample depths, by utilizing a handheld open-mouth bottle. Concurrent discharge measurements made at the streamflow sites followed the methods of Rantz and others (1982).

The USGS National Water-Quality Laboratory in Denver, Colorado, analyzed all fixed-station samples for dissolved and whole-water constituents using standard USGS methods and quality-assurance practices (Fishman and Friedman, 1989; Patton and Truitt, 1992; Fishman, 1993). For a few samples, a discrepancy was noted where total unfiltered organic nitrogen reported a lower value than filtered organic nitrogen, even after accounting for error margins on reporting limits. Multiple analyses of affected samples validated these results. A summary of the standard analytical methods used and associated references are provided in table 2. Analytical results for each fixed station are presented in table 9 (at back of report) and table 3.

Table 2. Summary of standard analytical methods and associated references.

[**Parameter**: Dis fet lab, dissolved fixed end point laboratory analysis; Dis tot IT field, dissolved total incremental titration. **Abbreviations**: °C, degrees Celsius; USGS, U.S. Geological Survey; CaCO$_3$, calcium carbonate]

Parameter	Publication	Method of analysis
Solids, residue, dissolved	Fishman and others (1994)	Gravimetric, residue on evaporation at 180°C
Turbidity	Fishman and Friedman (1989)	Nephelometry
Oxygen, dissolved	USGS (1997–99)	Amperometric
pH, whole water	USGS (1997–99)	Electrometric electrode
Specific conductance	USGS (1997–99)	Wheatstone Bridge
Major ions		
Calcium, dissolved	Fishman (1993)	Inductively Coupled Plasma–Atomic Emission Spectrometry
Magnesium, dissolved	Fishman (1993)	Inductively Coupled Plasma–Atomic Emission Spectrometry
Potassium, dissolved	Fishman and Friedman (1989)	Flame atomic absorption
Sodium, dissolved	Fishman (1993)	Inductively Coupled Plasma–Atomic Emission Spectrometry
Alkalinity, Dis fet lab, as CaCO$_3$	USGS (1997–99)	Dissolved fixed end point titration
Alkalinity, Dis tot IT, field	USGS (1997–99)	Dissolved incremental end point titration
Bicarbonate Dis IT, field	USGS (1997–99)	Calculated
Chloride, dissolved	Fishman and Friedman (1989)	Ion chromatography
Fluoride, dissolved	Fishman and Friedman (1989)	Automated segmented flow-ion-selective electrode
Silica, dissolved	Fishman (1993)	Inductively Coupled Plasma–Atomic Emission Spectrometry
Sulfate, dissolved	Fishman and Friedman (1989)	Ion chromatography
Nutrients		
Nitrogen, ammonia, dissolved	Fishman (1993)	Colorimetry, automated segmented flow–salicylate-hypochlorite
Nitrogen, ammonia+organic, dissolved	Patton and Truitt (2000)	Colorimetry, automated segmented flow–Microkjeldahl digestion
Nitrogen, ammonia+organic, total	Fishman and others (1994)	Colorimetry, block digestor salicylate-hypochlorite
Nitrogen, nitrite+nitrate, dissolved	Fishman (1993)	Colorimetry, automated segmented flow–cadmium reduction-diazotization
Nitrogen, nitrate, dissolved	Fishman and Friedman (1989)	Ion chromatography
Phosphorus, dissolved	Patton and Truitt (1992)	Colorimetry, automated segmented flow–Microkjeldahl digestion
Orthophosphorus	Fishman (1993)	Colorimetry, automated segmented flow–phosphomolybdate
Phosphorus, total	Patton and Truitt (1992)	Colorimetry, automated segmented flow–Microkjeldahl digestion
Carbon, organic, dissolved (DOC)	Brenton and Arnett (1993)	Wet-chemical oxidation, nondispersive infrared detector
Trace elements		
Iron, dissolved	Fishman (1993)	Inductively Coupled Plasma–Atomic Emission Spectrometry
Manganese, dissolved	Faires (1993)	Inductively Coupled Plasma–Mass Spectrometry

Table 3. Concentrations of selected major ions, nutrients and trace elements in water samples from streamflow sampling sites, Denali National Park and Preserve and surrounding area, Alaska.

[Location of sampling sites are shown in figure 2. Parameters: Dis fet lab, Dissolved fixed end-point titration in laboratory; Dis tot IT Field, Dissolved total Incremental Titration in the field; Dis IT Field, Dissolved Incremental Titration in the field FNU, Formazin Nephelometric Unit; Hg, mercury; $CaCO_3$, calcium carbonate; NO_2, nitrite; NO_3, nitrate; E, estimated value. <, less than detection limit; m^3/s, cubic meter per second; m, meter; mm, millimeter; mL, milliliter; mg/L, milligram per liter; μS/cm, microsiemen per centimeter at 25 degrees Celsius; C, Celsius; –, missing value]

USGS site No.	Date	Time	Discharge (m^3/s) 00061	Stream width (m) 00004	Turbidity, field, YSI (FNU) 63680	Barometric pressure (mm of Hg) 00025	Oxygen, dissolved (mg/L) 00300	pH, field (units) 00400	pH, laboratory (units) 00403	Specific conductance, laboratory (μS/cm) 90095	Specific conductance, field (μS/cm) 00095	Air temperature (°C) 00020	Water temperature (°C) 00020
6329441505320000	06-27-07	1715	0.065	2.1	<1	716	10.0	7.9	8.4	204	199	–	17.6
6329451505301000	06-27-07	1745	E 0.028	E 0.46	12.2	716	10.1	7.5	7.5	331	324	–	16.5

USGS site No.	Date	Time	Calcium (mg/L) 00915	Magnesium (mg/L) 00925	Potassium (mg/L) 00935	Sodium (mg/L) 00930	Alkalinity, Dis fet Lab, as $CaCO_3$ (mg/L) 39086	Alkalinity, Dis tot IT Field (mg/L) 29801	Bicarbonate, Dis IT Field (mg/L) 00453	Fluoride (mg/L) 00950	Silica, (mg/L) 00955
6329441505320000	06-27-07	1715	33.0	4.28	0.77	1.18	92	84	102	<0.10	3.56
6329451505301000	06-27-07	1745	52.3	8.81	1.11	1.80	150	141	172	E 0.06	6.73

USGS site No.	Date	Time	Solids, residue at 180°C, dissolved (mg/L) 70300	Sulfate (mg/L) 00945	Nitrogen, ammonia + organic, dissolved (mg/L) 00623	Nitrogen, ammonia + organic, total (mg/L) 00625	Nitrogen, ammonia, dissolved (mg/L) 00608	Nitrogen, NO_2+NO_3, dissolved (mg/L) 00631	Nitrogen, nitrite, dissolved (mg/L) 00613	Ortho-phosphorus (mg/L) 00671	Phosphorus (mg/L) 00666	Phosphorus, total (mg/L) 00665
6329441505320000	06-27-07	1715	118	14.9	0.12	0.16	<0.020	0.018	<0.002	<0.006	<0.006	<0.008
6329451505301000	06-27-07	1745	191	26.2	0.53	0.17	<0.020	0.121	<0.002	E 0.003	<0.006	E 0.006

USGS site No.	Date	Time	Carbon, organic (mg/L) 00681	Iron (μg/L) 01046	Manganese (μg/L) 01056
6329441505320000	06-27-07	1715	2.1	E 5	1.5
6329451505301000	06-27-07	1745	2.4	15	28.6

Continuous-Record Water Temperature Profiles

A single line anchor/buoy system was used to install self-recording temperature sensors at multiple depths at Wonder Lake Site 2, at Chilchukabena Lake, and Lake Minchumina (fig. 5). The sensor strings were emplaced through ice cover during April 2007. The Wonder Lake string was pulled, downloaded, and re-installed in June 2007 and again in August 2007, along with those from Chilchukabena Lake and Lake Minchumina. During the winter of 2007–08, the sensor strings froze into the ice cover, drifting an indeterminate amount as the ice cover shifted during spring thaw. The Wonder and Chilchukabena Lake strings were recovered in autumn 2008 about 60 m from their original location, but the Lake Minchumina sensor string was not found. Temperature record for all sites was excellent (95 percent of the record is within 5 percent of the true value) from April 2007 through April 2008. Wonder Lake temperature record from May 2008 through August 2008 was downgraded to good (95 percent of the record is within 10 percent of the true value) for sensor drift errors (errors mitigated by profile data showing good lateral homogeneity in the water column). Chilchukabena Lake temperature record for May 2008 through June 2008 was downgraded to poor (may have less than 95 percent of the record within 15 percent of the true value) for sensor drift errors (lake was very shallow compared to Wonder Lake and there is no corroborating evidence for lateral homogeneity in the water column). Daily value temperature data related to depth is presented graphically in figures 6A-6C. Original data are available from the USGS NWIS database (http://waterdata.usgs.gov/ak/nwis/).

Figure 5.   Buoys, sensors, and anchor used to measure temperature in Wonder Lake, Chilchukabena Lake and Lake Minchumina, Alaska. Photograph taken by Daniel A. Long , 2007.

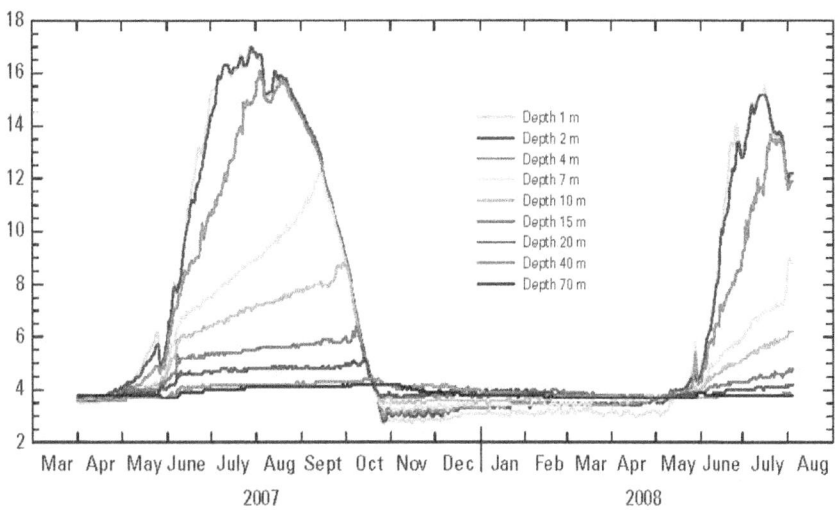

A. Wonder Lake Site 2 Continuous Temperature Profile

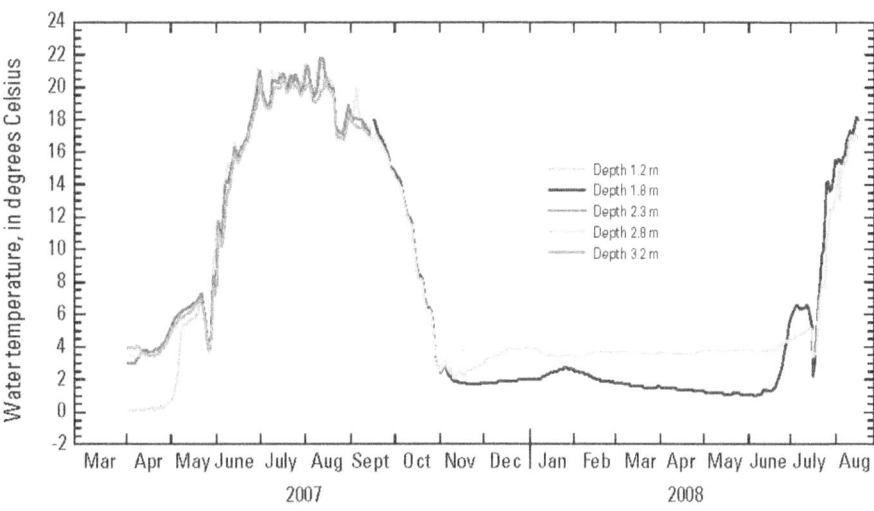

B. Chilchukabena Lake Continuous Temperature Profile

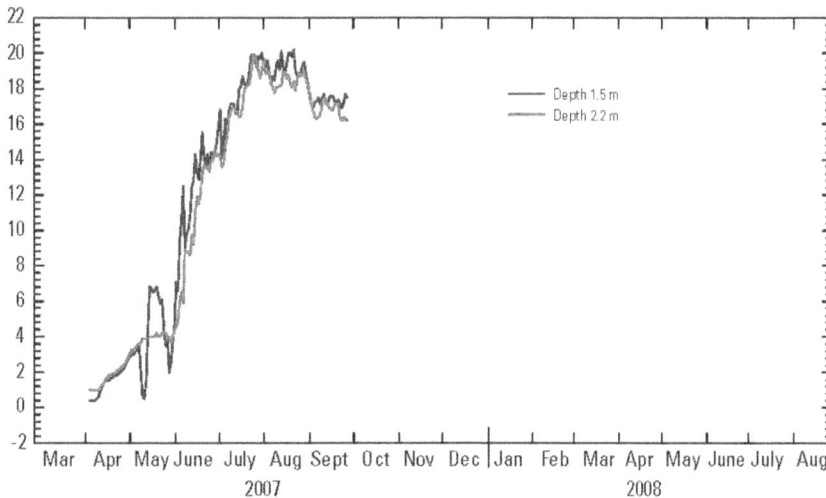

C. Lake Minchumina Continuous Temperature Profile

Figure 6.   Temperature profiles for Wonder Lake, Chilchukabena Lake, and Lake Minchumina, in Denali National Park and Preserve, Alaska.

Zooplankton Sampling

Zooplankton samples were collected at sites 1–3 from Wonder Lake in June, July, and September 2006. Vertical tows began 2 m above the lake bottom using a 0.5-m diameter, 153-µm mesh, conical plankton net pulled at 0.6 m/s. Samples were preserved in 10 percent buffered formalin.

Taxonomic identification and density of phytoplankton was obtained following standard methods (Ward and Whipple, 1918; Balcer and others, 1984). Preserved zooplankton samples were concentrated by gently pouring the original sample (about 125–200 mL) through a 153–µm mesh, followed by resuspension into about 65 mL 4-percent formalin (final concentration). One to two 2-mL subsamples were enumerated by low power microscopy (dissecting microscope) to obtain approximately 100 total organisms in each subsample. Broad groupings of zooplankton were enumerated. Daphnia, Bosmina, and Ceriodaphnia were enumerated (of the cladoceran group of zooplankton). Calanoida and cyclopoid copepods, and nauplii larvae were enumerated (of the copepod zooplankton). Net diameter and depth and number of tows were factored in when calculating the number of organisms per cubic meter of water sampled. Zooplankton data are presented in table 4.

Snow Sampling

A single snow sample was collected from Wonder Lake site 4 on April 23, 2006 (fig. 2) following WACAP procedures (Landers and others, 2008). Snow was collected as a vertically integrated sample from a snowpit wall using polycarbonate scoops, placed in Teflon™ bags, and frozen for shipping. Results of sample analysis for semivolatile organic compounds (SVOCs), trace elements, and mercury are shown in tables 5-7.

Table 4.   Analysis of zooplankton in water samples from sampling sites 1–3, Wonder Lake, Denali National Park and Preserve, Alaska.

[Location of sampling sites are shown in figure 2]

Sampling site No.	Date	Cladocerans		Copepods					Total counts	Total organisms per cubic meter
		Bosmina	Daphnia	Cyclopoid1	Cyclopoid2	Calanoid1	Calanoid2	Nauplii		
1	06-20-06	2	1	17	0	18	0	64	102	275
2	06-20-06	0	1	47	0	16	0	98	162	41
3	06-20-06	14	1	39	0	33	0	70	157	276
1	07-25-06	3	0	200	0	419	0	235	857	107
2	07-25-06	0	0	77	0	22	1	13	113	157
3	07-25-06	1	0	278	0	266	1	130	676	26
1	09-07-06	10	0	125	0	78	7	14	234	6
2	09-07-06	1	0	128	1	50	1	92	273	2,194
3	09-07-06	27	1	56	1	96	1	5	187	498

Table 5. Analysis of semi-volatile organic compounds in a snow sample from Wonder Lake site 4, Denali National Park and Preserve, Alaska, April 26, 2006.

[Single snow sample collected at Wonder Lake (site 4). USGS site No. 632937150525600; elevation, 610 meters above National Geodetic Vertical Datum of 1929; WACAP No. 66873. WACAP, Western Airborne Contaminants Assessment Project. Location of sampling site is shown in figure 2. –, missing value. **Flag:**

a   Detected but below the quantification limit. The quantification limit equals the concentration of the lowest calibration standard at which the signal to noise ratio is greater than or equal to 10.

b   Above the calibration range; that is, greater than the concentration of the highest calibration standard used to make the calibration curve.

c   Performance standard deviated by >30 percent

d   Surrogate recovery <30 or >130 percent

e   Laboratory blank >5 percent

f   Field blank >20 percent

X   Do not use because laboratory blank was >33 percent of the value]

Compound	Concentration	Flag	Compound	Concentration	Flag
Matrix: Concentration, in nanograms per liter			Matrix: Concentration, in nanograms per liter		
Acenaphthene	-0.011		g-Hexaclorcyclohexane	-0.011	
Acenaphthylene	-0.02		Hexachlorobenzene	0.019	e,f
Acetochlor	-0.025		Heptachlor	-0.023	
a-Hexachlorcyclohexane	-0.017		Heptachlor epoxide	-0.008	
Alachlor	-0.043		Indeno(1,2,3-cd)pyrene	-0.032	
Aldrin	-0.073		Malathion	-0.008	
Anthracene	-0.02		Metribuzin	-0.003	
Atrazine	-0.012		Methoxychlor	-0.016	
Benzo(a)anthracene	-0.015		Methyl parathion	-0.052	
Benzo(a)pyrene	-0.008		Metolachlor	-0.014	
Benzo(b)fluoranthene	-0.007		Mirex	-0.010	
Benzo(e)pyrene	-0.009		o,p'-DDD	-0.025	
Benzo(ghi)perylene	-0.017		o,p'-DDE	-0.025	
Benzo(k)fluoranthene	-0.005		o,p'-DDT	-0.023	
b-Hexachlorcyclohexane	-0.026		o-CLDN	-0.002	
cis-Chlordane	-0.005		p,p'-DDD	-0.044	
Chrysene +Triphenylene	-0.013		p,p'-DDE	-0.01	
Chlorpyrifos	0.018	e,f	p,p'-DDT	-0.026	
Chlorpyrifos oxon	-0.058		Parathion	-0.003	
cis-Nonachlor	0.002	a	PCB101	-0.012	
Cyanazine	-0.026		PCB118	–	e,f,X
Dacthal	0.006	c,e	PCB138	–	e,f,X
d-Hexachlorcyclohexane	-0.008		PCB153	–	e,f,X
Diazinon	-0.009		PCB183	0.002	e,f
Dibenz(a,h)anthracene	-0.029		PCB187	–	e,f,X
Dieldrin	-0.014		PCB74	-0.18	
Endosulfan I	0.039		Pebulate	-0.064	
Endosulfan II	-0.002		Phenanthrene	0.66	e,f
Endosulfan sulfate	0.15	c	Prometon	-0.035	
Endrin	-0.06		Propachlor	-0.004	
Endrin aldehyde	-0.005		Pyrene	-0.005	
EPTC	-0.045		Retene	0.34	
Ethion	-0.006		trans-Chlordane	0.002	a
Etridiazole	-0.023		Trifluralin	0.004	d,e,f
Fluoranthene	-0.004		trans-Nonachlor	0.004	c
Fluorene	–	efX	Triallate	-0.007	

Table 5.   Analysis of semi-volatile organic compounds in a snow sample from Wonder Lake site 4, Denali National Park and Preserve, Alaska, April 26, 2006.—Continued

[Single snow sample collected at Wonder Lake (site 4). USGS site No. 632937150525600; elevation, 610 meters above National Geodetic Vertical Datum of 1929; WACAP No. 66873. WACAP, Western Airborne Contaminants Assessment Project. Location of sampling site is shown in figure 2. –, missing value.
Flag:

a   Detected but below the quantification limit. The quantification limit equals the concentration of the lowest calibration standard at which the signal to noise ratio is greater than or equal to 10.
b   Above the calibration range; that is, greater than the concentration of the highest calibration standard used to make the calibration curve.
c   Performance standard deviated by >30 percent
d   Surrogate recovery <30 or >130 percent
e   Laboratory blank >5 percent
f   Field blank >20 percent
X   Do not use because laboratory blank was >33 percent of the value]

Compound	Concentration	Flag	Compound	Concentration	Flag
Matrix: FLUX, nanograms per square meter			Matrix: FLUX, nanograms per square meter		
Acenaphthene	-1.2		g-Hexachlorcyclohexane	-1.1	
Acenaphthylene	-2		Hexachlorobenzene	1.9	e,f
Acetochlor	-2.6		Heptachlor	-2.4	
a-Hexachlorcyclohexane	-1.7		Heptachlor epoxide	-0.87	
Alachlor	-4.5		Indeno(1,2,3-cd)pyrene	-3.2	
Aldrin	-7.5		Malathion	-0.87	
Anthracene	-2.1		Metribuzin	-0.32	
Atrazine	-1.2		Methoxychlor	-1.7	
Benzo(a)anthracene	-1.5		Methyl parathion	-5.4	
Benzo(a)pyrene	-0.81		Metolachlor	-1.4	
Benzo(b)fluoranthene	-0.71		Mirex	-1	
Benzo(e)pyrene	-0.92		o,p'-DDD	-2.5	
Benzo(ghi)perylene	-1.7		o,p'-DDE	-2.5	
Benzo(k)fluoranthene	-0.52		o,p'-DDT	-2.4	
b-Hexachlorcyclohexane	-2.7		Chlordane, oxy	-0.19	
cis-Chlordane	-0.52		p,p'-DDD	-4.5	
Chrysene +Triphenylene	-1.4		p,p'-DDE	-1.1	
Chlorpyrifos	1.8	e,f	p,p'-DDT	-2.7	
Chlorpyrifos oxon	-6		Parathion	-0.33	
cis-Nonachlor	0.25	a	PCB101	-1.3	
Cyanazine	-2.7		PCB118	–	e,f,X
Dacthal	0.58	c,e	PCB138	–	e,f,X
d-Hexachlorcyclohexane	-0.81		PCB153	–	e,f,X
Diazinon	-0.94		PCB183	0.21	e,f
Dibenz(a,h)anthracene	-3		PCB187	–	e,f,X
Dieldrin	-1.4		PCB74	-18	
Endosulfan I	4		Pebulate	-6.6	
Endosulfan II	-0.2		Phenanthrene	68	e,f
Endosulfan sulfate	16	c	Prometon	-3.6	
Endrin	-6.2		Propachlor	-0.38	
Endrin A	-0.56		Pyrene	-0.51	
EPTC	-4.6		Retene	35	
Ethion	-0.64		trans-Chlordane	0.24	a
Etridiazole	-2.3		Trifluralin	0.41	d,e,f
Fluoranthene	-0.41		trans-Nonachlor	0.41	c
Fluorene	–	e,f,X	Triallate	-0.7	

Table 6. Analysis of trace elements, filtered, dissolved in a snow sample from Wonder Lake site 4, Denali National Park and Preserve, Alaska, April 26, 2006.

[Single snow sample collected at Wonder Lake (site 4). USGS site No. 632937150525600; sample date, April 26, 2006; sample time 15:00; elevation, 610 meters above National Geodetic Vertical Datum of 1929; WACAP No. 66873. WACAP, Western Airborne Contaminants Assessment Project. Location of sampling site is shown in figure 2. SD, standard deviation; µg/L, micrograms per liter; mg/L, milligrams per liter; <, less than]

Element	Average	SD
Aluminum, µg/L	2.1	0.1
Arsenic, µg/L	0.050	0.003
Barium, µg/L	1.4	0.0
Beryllium, µg/L	0.005	0.000
Bismuth, µg/L	< 0.002	0.000
Boron, µg/L	0.5	0.1
Cadmium, µg/L	0.028	0.003
Calcium, mg/L	0.46	0.00
Cerium, µg/L	0.003	0.001
Cesium, µg/L	0.002	0.002
Chromium, µg/L	< 0.05	0.03
Cobalt, µg/L	0.13	0.01
Copper, µg/L	0.12	0.00
Dysprosium, µg/L	< 0.001	0.000
Erbium, µg/L	< 0.001	0.000
Europium, µg/L	0.000	0.000
Gadolinium, µg/L	0.000	0.000
Holmium, µg/L	< 0.000	0.000
Iron, µg/L	< 4	0
Lanthanum, µg/L	0.001	0.000
Lead, µg/L	0.027	0.003
Lithium, µg/L	0.047	0.012
Lutetium, µg/L	< 0.000	0.000
Magnesium, mg/L	0.040	0.000
Manganese, µg/L	7.0	0.2
Molybdenum, µg/L	0.10	0.06
Neodymium, µg/L	0.003	0.002
Nickel, µg/L	0.20	0.01
Phosphorus, µg/L	< 4	1
Potassium, mg/L	0.008	0.003
Praseodymium, µg/L	0.000	0.000
Rhenium, µg/L	< 0.000	0.000
Rubidium, µg/L	0.030	0.001
Samarium, µg/L	< 0.000	0.001
Selenium, µg/L	< 0.05	0.01
Silica, mg/L	< 0.04	0.03
Sodium, mg/L	0.10	0.01
Strontium, µg/L	1.6	0.0
Sulfur, mg/L	0.12	0.02
Tellurium, µg/L	< 0.004	0.001
Terbium, µg/L	< 0.000	0.000
Thallium, µg/L	< 0.01	0.00
Thulium, µg/L	< 0.000	0.000
Tungsten, µg/L	< 0.001	0.000
Uranium, µg/L	0.003	0.001
Vanadium, µg/L	0.04	0.02
Ytterbium, µg/L	0.000	0.000
Yttrium, µg/L	0.003	0.000
Zinc, µg/L	1.1	0.0
Zirconium, µg/L	0.009	0.006

Table 7. Analysis of mercury in a snow sample from Wonder Lake site 4, Denali National Park and Preserve, Alaska, April 26, 2006.

[Single snow sample collected at Wonder Lake (site 4). USGS site No. 632937150525600; sample date, April 26, 2006; sample time 15:00; elevation, 610 meters above National Geodetic Vertical Datum of 1929; WACAP No. 66873. WACAP, Western Airborne Contaminants Assessment Project. Location of sampling site is shown in figure 2. $CaCO_3$, calcium carbonate; μeq/L, micro-equivalent per liter; μS/cm, microsiemen per centimenter at 25 degrees Celsius; μmol/L, micromole per liter; cm, centimeter; ng/L, nanogram per liter]

Alkalinity, as CaCO3 (μeq/L)	Specific conductance (μS/cm)	pH, laboratory	Hydrogen ion (from pH)	Calcium (μeq/L)	Magnesium (μeq/L)	Sodium (μeq/L)
7.2	5.9	6.07	0.851	19.46	2.46	4.23

Potassium (μeq/L)	Ammonia (μmol/L)	Silica (μmol/L)	Chloride (μeq/L)	Sulfate (μeq/L)	Nitrate (μmol/L)
0.27	1.25	0.49	14.95	7.21	2.03

Strontium (μeq/L)	Dissolved organic carbon (mg/L)	Ultraviolet absorption (nm)	Snow depth (cm)	Snow water equivalent (cm)	Total mercury (ng/L)
0.023	0	0.003	40	10	3.69

References Cited

Alaska Division of Community and Regional Affairs, 2010, Alaska Community Database Community Information Summaries (CIS) Lake Minchumina: http://www.commerce.state.ak.us/dca/comndb/CF_CIS.htm, (accessed February 8, 2010).

Balcer, B.D., Korda, N.L., and Dodson, S.I., 1984, Zooplankton of the Great Lakes: London, England, The University of Wisconsin Press, Ltd., p. 56-58.

Brenton, R.W., and Arnett, T.L., 1993, Methods of analysis by the U.S. Geological Survey National Water Quality Laboratory—Determination of dissolved organic carbon by UV-promoted persulfate oxidation and infrared spectrometry: U.S. Geological Survey Open-File Report 92-480, 12 p.

Child, J.K., 1995, A Late Quaternary lacustrine record of environmental change in the Wonder Lake area, Denali National Park and Preserve, Alaska: Amherst, University of Massachusetts, M.S. Thesis, 205 p.

Faires, L.M., 1993, Methods of analysis by the U.S. Geological Survey National Water Quality Laboratory—Determination of metals in water by inductively coupled plasma mass-spectrometry: U.S. Geological Survey Open-File Report 92-634, 28 p.

Fishman, M.J., ed., 1993, Methods of analysis by the U.S. Geological Survey National Water Quality Laboratory—Determination of inorganic and organic constituents in water and fluvial sediments: U.S. Geological Survey Open-File Report 93-125, 217 p.

Fishman, M.J., and Friedman, L.C., eds., 1989, Methods for determination of inorganic substances in water and fluvial sediments: U.S. Geological Survey Techniques of Water-Resources Investigations, book 5, chap. A1, 545 p.

Fishman, M.J., Raese, J.W., Gerlitz, C.N., and Husband, R.A., 1994, U.S. Geological Survey approved inorganic and organic methods for the analysis of water and fluvial sediment, 1954-94: U.S. Geological Survey Open-File Report 94-351, 55 p.

Horowitz, A.J., Demas, C.R., Fitzgerald, K.K., Miller, T.L., and Rickert, D.A.,, 1994, U.S. Geological Survey protocol for the collection and processing of surface-water samples for the subsequent determination of inorganic constituents in filtered water: U.S. Geological Survey Open-File Report 94-539, 57 p.

Kodama, Y., Eaton, F., and Wendler, G., 1983, The influence of Lake Minchumina, Interior Alaska, on its surroundings: Archives for Meterology, Geophysics, and Bioclimatology Series B, v. 33, issue 3, p. 199-218.

Landers, D.H., Simonich, S.L., Jaffe, D.A., Geiser, L.H., Campbell, D.H., Schwindt, A.R., Schreck, C.B., Kent, M.L., Hafner, W.D., Taylor, H.E., Hageman, K.J., Usenko, S., Ackerman, L.K., Schrlau, J.E., Rose, N.L., Blett, T.F., and Erway, M.M., 2008, The fate, transport, and ecological impacts of airborne contaminants in Western National Parks (USA): EPA/600/R-07/138. U.S. Environmental Protection Agency, Office of Research and Development, NHEERL, Western Ecology Division, Corvallis, Ore

Laperriere, J., and Casper, L., 1976, Biogeochemistry of deep lakes in the central Alaska Range: University of Alaska, Fairbanks Institute of Water Resources Report No. IWR-68, 35 p.

Patton, C.J., and Truitt, E.P., 1992, Methods of analysis by the U.S. Geological Survey National Water Quality Laboratory—Determination of total phosphorus by a Kjeldahl digestion method and an automated colorimetric finish that includes dialysis: U.S. Geological Survey Open-File Report 92-146, 39 p.

Patton, C.J., and Truitt, E.P., 2000, Methods of analysis by the U.S. Geological Survey National Water Quality Laboratory—Determination of ammonium plus organic nitrogen by a Kjeldahl digestion method and an automated photometric finish that includes digest cleanup by gas diffusion: U.S. Geological Survey Open-File Report 00-170, 31 p.

Rantz, S.E., and others, 1982, Measurement and computation of streamflow: Volume 1. Measurement of stage and discharge: U.S. Geological Survey Water-Supply Paper 2175, 313 p.

U.S. Geological Survey, variously dated, National field manual for the collection of water-quality data: U.S. Geological Survey Techniques of Water-Resources Investigations, book 9, chaps. A1-A9. (Also available at http://pubs.water.usgs.gov/twri9A.)

Ward, H.B., and Whipple, G.C., 1918, Fresh Water Biology, Second Edition: Edmondson, W.T., ed.: New York, John Wiley & Sons, Inc., 1248 p.

Werner, A., 1990, Bathymetry and stratigraphy of Wonder Lake, a glacial lake in Denali National Park and Preserve, Alaska: Research Summary, Mount Holyoke College, South Hadley, 23 p.

Table 8. Field parameters for lake water-quality samples from Wonder Lake, Chilchukabena Lake, and Lake Minchumina, Denali National Park and Preserve and surrounding area, Alaska.

[Location of sampling sites are shown in figure 2. FNU, Formazin Nephelometric Unit; <, less then detection limit; m, meter; mg/L, milligram per liter; μS/cm, microsiemen per centimeter at 25 degrees Celsius; C, Celsius; –, missing value]

Date	Time	Depth sample (m) 00098	Turbidity, field YSI (FNU) 63680	Oxygen, dissolved (mg/L) 00300	pH, field 00400	Specific conductance, field (μS/cm) 00095	Water temperature (°C) 00020	Phyto-plankton, chlorophyll uncorrected (mg/L) 32234
				Wonder Lake Site 1				
06-20-06	0910	1	<1	10.3	8.2	196	12.4	2.3
	0912	2	<1	10.3	8.2	196	12.4	1.1
	0914	3	<1	10.4	8.2	197	11.9	1.0
	0916	4	<1	10.6	8.1	197	10.8	1.6
	0918	5	<1	10.7	8.1	198	9.9	1.4
	0920	6	<1	10.8	8.0	198	9.0	1.4
	0922	7	<1	10.9	8.0	199	7.8	2.5
	0924	8	<1	10.8	8.0	200	7.2	1.9
	0926	9	<1	10.8	8.0	200	7.0	3.1
	0928	10	<1	10.7	7.9	200	6.6	3.0
	0930	11	<1	10.7	7.9	201	6.2	2.8
	0932	12	<1	10.7	7.9	202	5.7	2.8
	0934	13	<1	10.0	7.9	204	5.5	–
07-25-06	0940	0	<1	9.9	8.3	196	16.0	1.4
	0942	1	<1	9.7	8.3	196	16.0	1.1
	0944	2	<1	9.7	8.3	196	16.0	1.5
	0946	3	<1	9.7	8.3	196	16.0	1.4
	0948	4	<1	9.7	8.3	196	16.0	1.2
	0950	5	<1	9.7	8.3	196	16.0	1.3
	0952	6	<1	9.7	8.3	196	15.8	2.1
	0954	7	<1	10.9	8.3	199	12.1	2.0
	0956	8	<1	11.5	8.2	202	9.0	1.7
	0958	9	<1	11.5	8.2	202	8.0	2.5
	1000	10	<1	11.4	8.1	202	7.4	2.4
	1002	11	<1	11.3	8.1	203	6.7	3.0
	1004	12	<1	11.2	8.0	204	6.2	3.5
	1006	13	<1	11.0	8.0	205	5.8	3.9
	1008	14	<1	10.8	7.9	205	5.6	3.9
	1010	15	<1	10.7	7.9	206	5.4	3.9
	1012	16	<1	10.6	7.8	206	5.3	4.1
	1014	17	<1	10.5	7.8	207	5.1	3.2
	1016	18	<1	10.3	7.8	209	4.6	3.4
09-07-06	0930	0.1	<1	10.7	8.3	194	11.5	0.5
	0932	1	<1	10.6	8.3	194	11.5	0.8
	0934	2	<1	10.6	8.3	194	11.5	0.7
	0936	3	<1	10.6	8.3	194	11.5	1.5
	0938	4	<1	10.6	8.3	194	11.5	0.5
	0940	5	<1	10.6	8.3	194	11.5	0.6
	0942	6	<1	10.5	8.3	194	11.4	1.8
	0944	7	<1	10.5	8.3	194	11.4	0.5
	0946	8	<1	10.5	8.3	194	11.4	0.3
	0948	9	<1	10.6	8.3	195	11.2	0.7
	0950	10	<1	11.5	8.3	202	8.9	1.5
	0952	11	<1	11.7	8.2	203	7.6	1.4
	0954	12	<1	11.5	8.2	203	7.0	2.0
	0956	13	<1	11.4	8.1	204	6.5	3.2
	958	14	<1	11.3	8.1	205	6.2	3.2

Table 8   19

Table 8. Field parameters for lake water-quality samples from Wonder Lake, Chilchukabena Lake, and Lake Minchumina, Denali National Park and Preserve and surrounding area, Alaska.—Continued

[Location of sampling sites are shown in figure 2. FNU, Formazin Nephelometric Unit; <, less then detection limit; m, meter; mg/L, milligram per liter; µS/cm, microsiemen per centimeter at 25 degrees Celsius; C, Celsius; –, missing value]

Date	Time	Depth sample (m) 00098	Turbidity, field YSI (FNU) 63680	Oxygen, dissolved (mg/L) 00300	pH, field 00400	Specific conductance, field (µS/cm) 00095	Water temperature (°C) 00020	Phyto-plankton, chlorophyll uncorrected (mg/L) 32234
				Wonder Lake Site 1—Continued				
09-07-06	1000	15	<1	11.0	8.0	205	5.9	3.5
	1002	16	<1	10.4	7.9	206	5.4	2.4
	1004	17	<1	10.5	7.8	206	5.4	2.2
	1006	18	<1	10.2	7.7	208	4.9	1.6
	1008	18.5	<1	10.1	7.7	209	4.7	2.0
				Wonder Lake Site 2				
06-20-06	1020	0	<1	10.4	8.2	196	11.6	1.1
	1021	1	<1	10.4	8.1	196	11.5	0.7
	1022	2	<1	10.4	8.2	196	11.5	0.9
	1023	3	<1	10.4	8.2	197	11.4	1.0
	1024	4	<1	10.6	8.1	198	10.4	2.0
	1025	5	<1	10.9	8.1	198	8.6	2.1
	1026	6	<1	10.9	8.0	199	7.8	2.1
	1027	7	<1	10.9	8.0	199	7.3	1.5
	1028	8	<1	10.9	8.0	200	6.7	2.1
	1029	9	<1	10.9	8.0	201	6.0	2.6
	1030	10	<1	10.7	8.0	201	5.9	3.4
	1031	11	<1	10.6	8.0	202	5.8	3.6
	1032	12	<1	10.6	7.9	202	5.6	3.9
	1033	13	<1	10.5	7.9	203	5.3	4.1
	1034	14	<1	10.4	7.9	204	5.2	4.3
	1035	15	<1	10.3	7.9	201	5.1	4.3
	1036	16	<1	10.3	7.9	204	5.0	4.0.
	1037	17	<1	10.3	7.8	205	4.9	3.1
	1038	18	<1	10.1	7.8	206	4.7	2.1
	1039	19	<1	10.0	7.8	206	4.6	2.3
	1040	20	<1	10.0	7.8	207	4.5	2.6
	1041	22	<1	9.9	7.8	207	4.5	2.4
	1042	24	<1	9.9	7.8	208	4.3	2.4
	1043	26	<1	9.8	7.8	209	4.1	0.7
	1044	28	<1	9.6	7.8	210	4.1	1.7
	1045	30	<1	9.6	7.7	210	4.0	1.5
	1046	32	<1	9.5	7.7	210	4.0	1.3
	1047	34	<1	9.5	7.7	210	4.0	1.6
	1048	36	<1	9.4	7.7	211	3.9	1.6
	1049	38	<1	9.3	7.7	211	3.9	1.4
	1050	40	<1	9.3	7.7	211	3.9	1.4
	1051	42	<1	9.3	7.7	211	3.9	1.4
	1052	44	<1	9.3	7.7	211	3.9	0.9
	1053	46	<1	9.3	7.7	211	3.8	1.4
	1054	48	<1	9.2	7.7	211	3.8	1.1
	1055	50	<1	9.2	7.7	211	3.8	1.1
	1056	52	<1	9.2	7.7	212	3.8	1.5
	1057	54	<1	9.2	7.7	212	3.8	1.3
	1058	56	<1	9.1	7.7	212	3.8	1.2
	1059	58	<1	9.1	7.7	212	3.8	1.2
	1100	60	<1	9.1	7.7	212	3.8	1.1

Table 8.   Field parameters for lake water-quality samples from Wonder Lake, Chilchukabena Lake, and Lake Minchumina, Denali National Park and Preserve and surrounding area, Alaska.—Continued

[Location of sampling sites are shown in figure 2. FNU, Formazin Nephelometric Unit; <, less then detection limit; m, meter; mg/L, milligram per liter; µS/cm, microsiemen per centimeter at 25 degrees Celsius; C, Celsius; –, missing value]

Date	Time	Depth sample (m) 00098	Turbidity, field YSI (FNU) 63680	Oxygen, dissolved (mg/L) 00300	pH, field 00400	Specific conductance, field (µS/cm) 00095	Water temperature (°C) 00020	Phyto-plankton, chlorophyll uncorrected (mg/L) 32234
				Wonder Lake Site 2—Continued				
07-25-06	1200	0	<1	9.5	8.4	196	16.2	1.0
	1202	1	<1	9.5	8.3	196	16.2	1.0
	1204	2	<1	9.5	8.3	196	16.2	1.0
	1206	3	<1	9.5	8.3	196	16.2	1.0
	1208	4	<1	9.5	8.3	196	16.1	0.7
	1210	5	<1	9.6	8.4	196	16.0	1.4
	1212	6	<1	10.3	8.3	197	13.8	1.0
	1214	7	<1	10.6	8.3	198	12.7	2.0
	1216	8	<1	11.1	8.3	201	9.2	1.8
	1218	9	<1	11.1	8.2	202	7.5	2.0
	1220	10	<1	11.1	8.1	202	7.2	2.1
	1222	11	<1	11.1	8.1	203	7.0	2.8
	1224	12	<1	11.1	8.1	203	6.8	3.1
	1226	13	<1	11.1	8.1	204	6.3	3.4
	1228	14	<1	10.9	8.0	204	6.0	3.9
	1230	15	<1	10.9	8.0	205	5.7	4.0
	1232	16	<1	10.7	7.9	206	5.3	4.8
	1234	17	<1	10.4	7.9	206	5.1	4.5
	1236	18	<1	10.3	7.8	207	4.9	3.1
	1238	19	<1	10.1	7.8	208	4.7	3.4
	1240	20	<1	10.0	7.8	208	4.6	3.5
	1242	22	<1	9.9	7.7	209	4.5	3.6
	1246	24	<1	9.8	7.7	209	4.3	2.5
	1248	26	<1	9.7	7.7	210	4.2	2.0
	1250	28	<1	9.6	7.7	210	4.2	2.1
	1252	30	<1	9.7	7.6	210	4.2	2.1
	1254	35	<1	9.6	7.6	210	4.1	1.2
	1256	40	<1	9.6	7.6	211	4.0	1.6
	1258	45	<1	9.5	7.6	211	4.0	1.0
	1300	50	<1	9.5	7.6	212	4.0	1.4
	1302	55	<1	9.5	7.6	212	3.9	1.5
	1304	60	<1	9.4	7.6	212	3.9	1.2
09-07-06	1200	0.5	<1	10.4	8.3	194	11.5	0.5
	1202	1	<1	10.4	8.4	194	11.5	0.4
	1204	3	<1	10.4	8.4	194	11.5	0.5
	1206	5	<1	10.4	8.4	194	11.5	0.5
	1208	7	<1	10.4	8.4	194	11.3	1.1
	1210	8	<1	10.4	8.4	195	11.3	1.2
	1212	9	<1	10.6	8.4	196	11.0	1.3
	1214	10	<1	11.3	8.3	201	9.4	1.2
	1216	11	<1	11.6	8.3	202	8.0	1.2
	1218	12	<1	11.4	8.2	203	7.0	1.9
	1220	13	<1	11.3	8.2	204	6.7	2.2
	1222	14	<1	11.2	8.2	204	6.4	3.0
	1224	15	<1	11.1	8.1	204	6.2	3.2
	1226	17	<1	10.9	8.0	206	5.6	3.4
	1228	19	<1	10.4	7.8	207	5.1	2.0

Table 8   21

Table 8.   Field parameters for lake water-quality samples from Wonder Lake, Chilchukabena Lake, and Lake Minchumina, Denali National Park and Preserve and surrounding area, Alaska.—Continued

[Location of sampling sites are shown in figure 2. FNU, Formazin Nephelometric Unit; <, less then detection limit; m, meter; mg/L, milligram per liter; µS/cm, microsiemen per centimeter at 25 degrees Celsius; C, Celsius; –, missing value]

Date	Time	Depth sample (m) 00098	Turbidity, field YSI (FNU) 63680	Oxygen, dissolved (mg/L) 00300	pH, field 00400	Specific conductance, field (µS/cm) 00095	Water temperature (°C) 00020	Phytoplankton, chlorophyll uncorrected (mg/L) 32234
				Wonder Lake Site 2—Continued				
09-07-06	1230	21	<1	10.0	7.7	208	4.8	0.9
	1232	23	<1	10.1	7.7	209	4.5	1.0
	1234	25	<1	10.1	7.7	209	4.4	0.9
	1236	27	<1	10.0	7.6	210	4.3	0.9
	1238	30	<1	9.9	7.6	210	4.2	0.7
	1240	33	<1	9.9	7.6	210	4.1	0.1
	1242	37	<1	9.9	7.6	211	4.1	0.4
	1244	41	<1	9.8	7.6	211	4.0	0.1
	1246	45	<1	9.7	7.6	210	4.0	0.5
	1248	49	<1	9.7	7.6	211	4.0	0.9
	1250	53	<1	9.7	7.6	211	4.0	0.3
	1252	57	<1	9.7	7.6	211	3.9	0.7
	1254	60	<1	9.6	7.5	212	3.9	1.0
03-31-07	1338	0	<1	10.9	7.4	219	0.3	1.0
	1340	1	<1	10.1	7.5	208	3.5	1.0
	1342	2	<1	10.2	7.5	208	3.6	1.0
	1344	3	<1	10.2	7.5	208	3.6	1.1
	1346	4	<1	10.2	7.5	208	3.6	0.7
	1348	5	<1	10.2	7.5	209	3.6	1.2
	1350	6	<1	10.2	7.5	208	3.6	0.9
	1352	7	<1	10.2	7.5	208	3.6	1.3
	1354	8	<1	10.2	7.5	208	3.6	0.5
	1356	9	<1	10.2	7.5	208	3.6	0.9
	1358	14	<1	10.2	7.5	209	3.6	0.6
	1400	19	<1	10.2	7.5	208	3.6	0.9
	1402	24	<1	10.1	7.5	208	3.7	1.0
	1404	29	<1	10.0	7.5	209	3.7	0.5
	1406	34	<1	9.9	7.5	209	3.7	1.0
	1408	39	<1	9.9	–	209	3.7	0.7
	1410	44	<1	9.7	–	209	3.7	1.1
	1412	49	<1	9.8	–	210	3.7	0.5
	1414	54	<1	9.8	–	210	3.7	0.6
	1416	59	<1	9.8	–	210	3.6	0.7
06-26-07	1200	0.7	–	10.6	8.3	199	13.2	0.3
	1202	1	–	10.5	8.3	199	13.2	1.0
	1204	1.9	–	10.5	8.3	199	13.2	1.0
	1206	3	–	10.5	8.3	199	13.1	1.5
	1208	4.1	–	10.5	8.3	199	13.1	1.5
	1210	5.1	–	10.7	8.3	200	12.6	0.8
	1212	6	–	11.5	8.2	201	10.0	1.5
	1214	7	–	11.6	8.1	201	8.9	1.5
	1216	8.1	–	11.7	8.1	201	8.3	2.0
	1218	9.1	–	11.7	8.1	202	7.3	2.5
	1220	10	–	11.7	8.1	203	6.9	3.5
	1222	12	–	11.6	8.0	204	6.5	4.0
	1224	13.5	–	11.0	7.9	206	5.6	4.0
	1226	14	–	11.0	7.9	207	5.4	4.0

Table 8.   Field parameters for lake water-quality samples from Wonder Lake, Chilchukabena Lake, and Lake Minchumina, Denali National Park and Preserve and surrounding area, Alaska.—Continued

[Location of sampling sites are shown in figure 2. FNU, Formazin Nephelometric Unit; <, less then detection limit; m, meter; mg/L, milligram per liter; µS/cm, microsiemen per centimeter at 25 degrees Celsius; C, Celsius; –, missing value]

Date	Time	Depth sample (m) 00098	Turbidity, field YSI (FNU) 63680	Oxygen, dissolved (mg/L) 00300	pH, field 00400	Specific conductance, field (µS/cm) 00095	Water temperature (°C) 00020	Phyto-plankton, chlorophyll uncorrected (mg/L) 32234
				Wonder Lake Site 2—Continued				
06-26-07	1228	15.1	–	10.8	7.9	208	5.1	3.5
	1230	17	–	10.5	7.8	209	4.8	2.5
	1232	19	–	10.3	7.8	209	4.7	1.5
	1234	21.1	–	10.2	7.8	210	4.5	1.5
	1236	23.1	–	10.1	7.8	210	4.5	2.0
	1238	28.1	–	10.0	7.8	211	4.3	1.5
	1240	33.1	–	9.9	7.8	211	4.2	1.5
	1242	39.3	–	9.9	7.7	212	4.1	1.0
	1244	44.8	–	9.8	7.7	212	4.1	1.0
	1246	52.1	–	9.7	7.7	213	4.0	1.0
	1248	57.3	–	9.7	7.7	212	4.0	1.0
	1250	61.4	–	9.6	7.7	213	4.0	1.0
08-30-07	1208	0	<1	9.6	8.4	195	14.8	–
	1210	0.5	<1	9.6	8.4	195	14.7	–
	1212	1	<1	9.6	8.4	195	14.7	–
	1214	2	<1	9.6	8.4	195	14.6	–
	1216	3	<1	9.6	8.4	195	14.6	–
	1218	4	<1	9.6	8.4	195	14.6	–
	1220	5	<1	9.6	8.4	195	14.6	–
	1222	6	<1	9.6	8.4	195	14.5	–
	1224	7	<1	9.6	8.4	195	14.5	–
	1226	8	<1	9.6	8.4	196	14.4	–
	1228	9	<1	11.6	8.4	202	12.4	–
	1230	10	<1	12.2	8.4	203	10.0	–
	1232	11	<1	11.8	8.3	205	8.4	–
	1234	12	<1	11.8	8.3	205	7.9	–
	1236	13	<1	11.7	8.2	205	7.7	–
	1238	15	<1	11.4	8.1	206	6.9	–
	1240	18	<1	10.4	8.0	209	5.3	–
	1242	23	<1	9.7	7.9	210	4.8	–
	1244	28	<1	9.3	7.8	211	4.6	–
	1246	33	<1	9.0	7.8	211	4.4	–
	1248	38	<1	8.8	7.7	212	4.3	–
	1250	43	<1	8.7	7.7	212	4.2	–
	1252	48	<1	8.6	7.7	212	4.2	–
	1254	55	<1	8.6	7.7	212	4.2	–
	1256	62	<1	8.5	7.7	212	4.1	–
				Wonder Lake Site 3				
06-20-06	1210	0	<1	10.7	8.2	196	11.2	0.6
	1211	1	<1	10.6	8.2	196	11.2	1.1
	1212	2	<1	10.6	8.2	196	11.2	1.3
	1213	3	<1	10.6	8.2	197	11.1	1.4
	1214	4	<1	10.6	8.2	197	11.0	1.5
	1215	5	<1	10.8	8.1	198	10.2	2.0
	1216	6	<1	10.8	8.1	199	9.5	1.1
	1217	7	<1	11.0	8.1	199	8.1	1.1

Table 8   23

Table 8.   Field parameters for lake water-quality samples from Wonder Lake, Chilchukabena Lake, and Lake Minchumina, Denali National Park and Preserve and surrounding area, Alaska.—Continued

[Location of sampling sites are shown in figure 2. FNU, Formazin Nephelometric Unit; <, less then detection limit; m, meter; mg/L, milligram per liter; µS/cm, microsiemen per centimeter at 25 degrees Celsius; C, Celsius;   , missing value]

Date	Time	Depth sample (m) 00098	Turbidity, field YSI (FNU) 63680	Oxygen, dissolved (mg/L) 00300	pH, field 00400	Specific conductance, field (µS/cm) 00095	Water temperature (°C) 00020	Phyto-plankton, chlorophyll uncorrected (mg/L) 32234
				Wonder Lake Site 3—Continued				
06-20-06	1218	8	<1	10.9	8.1	199	7.8	2.0
	1219	9	<1	10.9	8.1	201	7.0	2.6
	1220	10	<1	10.9	8.0	201	6.6	2.2
	1221	11	<1	10.8	8.0	202	5.9	2.0
	1222	12	<1	10.7	8.0	203	5.6	2.1
	1223	13	<1	10.6	8.0	204	5.4	2.7
	1224	14	<1	10.4	7.9	204	5.4	3.0
	1225	15	<1	10.4	7.9	204	5.4	3.0
	1226	16	<1	11.0	8.0	205	5.0	0.9
	1227	17	<1	10.4	8.0	205	4.8	2.8
	1228	18	<1	10.2	8.0	205	4.8	2.8
	1229	19	<1	10.1	7.9	205	4.8	2.8
	1230	20	<1	10.0	7.9	206	4.8	2.6
07-25-06	1510	0	<1	10.2	8.4	196	16.0	1.8
	1512	1	<1	9.7	8.4	196	16.0	0.9
	1514	2	<1	9.6	8.4	196	16.0	1.5
	1516	3	<1	9.9	8.4	196	16.0	1.5
	1518	4	<1	9.9	8.4	196	16.0	2.0
	1520	5	<1	10.4	8.4	198	14.3	1.2
	1522	6	<1	11.2	8.3	199	12.2	1.8
	1524	7	<1	11.6	8.3	200	10.4	2.0
	1526	8	<1	11.7	8.2	201	9.9	2.3
	1528	9	<1	11.6	8.2	202	9.0	2.4
	1530	10	<1	11.5	8.2	202	7.9	2.3
	1532	11	<1	11.4	8.1	203	7.4	2.4
	1534	12	<1	11.4	8.1	203	7.0	2.9
	1536	13	<1	11.3	8.0	204	6.8	2.0
	1538	14	<1	11.2	8.0	204	6.7	3.8
	1540	15	<1	11.0	8.0	205	6.0	3.5
	1542	16	<1	10.9	7.9	206	5.4	4.1
	1544	17	<1	10.7	7.9	207	5.2	3.4
	1546	18	<1	10.6	7.8	207	5.1	3.5
	1548	19	<1	10.5	7.8	207	4.9	3.4
	1550	20	<1	10.4	7.8	208	4.9	4.0
	1552	21	<1	10.4	7.8	208	4.8	3.5
	1554	22	<1	10.3	7.7	208	4.6	3.0
	1556	23	<1	10.2	7.7	209	4.4	2.8
	1558	24	<1	10.0	7.7	209	4.4	2.9
09-07-06	1410	0.1	<1	12.0	8.4	194	11.3	0.2
	1412	0.5	<1	12.0	8.4	195	11.3	0.3
	1414	1	<1	11.8	8.4	195	11.3	0.5
	1416	2	<1	11.7	8.4	195	11.3	0.5
	1418	3	<1	11.6	8.4	195	11.3	0.5
	1420	4	<1	11.5	8.4	195	11.2	0.7
	1422	5	<1	11.4	8.4	195	11.2	0.4
	1424	6	<1	11.4	8.4	195	11.1	0.3
	1426	7	<1	11.3	8.4	195	11.1	0.4

Table 8. Field parameters for lake water-quality samples from Wonder Lake, Chilchukabena Lake, and Lake Minchumina, Denali National Park and Preserve and surrounding area, Alaska.—Continued

[Location of sampling sites are shown in figure 2. FNU, Formazin Nephelometric Unit; <, less then detection limit; m, meter; mg/L, milligram per liter; µS/cm, microsiemen per centimeter at 25 degrees Celsius; C, Celsius; –, missing value]

Date	Time	Depth sample (m) 00098	Turbidity, field YSI (FNU) 63680	Oxygen, dissolved (mg/L) 00300	pH, field 00400	Specific conductance, field (µS/cm) 00095	Water temperature (°C) 00020	Phyto-plankton, chlorophyll uncorrected (mg/L) 32234
				Wonder Lake Site 3—Continued				
09-07-06	1428	8	<1	11.3	8.4	195	11.0	0.8
	1430	9	<1	11.4	8.3	197	10.7	0.8
	1432	10	<1	12.2	8.2	202	8.1	1.6
	1434	11	<1	12.2	8.2	203	7.4	0.9
	1436	12	<1	11.9	8.1	204	6.7	1.1
	1438	13	<1	11.8	8.0	205	6.4	2.1
	1440	14	<1	11.4	7.9	206	5.8	1.4
	1442	15	<1	11.3	7.9	206	5.5	1.7
	1444	16	<1	11.1	7.8	208	5.0	1.6
	1446	17	<1	10.8	7.7	208	4.8	0.5
	1448	18	<1	10.7	7.7	208	4.7	1.5
	1450	19	<1	10.6	7.7	209	4.6	1.2
04-01-07	1300	0	<1	–	7.6	222	0.9	0.5
	1302	1	<1	–	7.6	215	3.1	0.2
	1304	2	<1	–	7.6	214	4.0	0.2
	1306	3	<1	–	7.6	214	3.5	0.7
	1308	4	<1	–	7.6	214	3.5	0.8
	1310	5	<1	–	7.6	214	3.5	0.3
	1312	6	<1	–	7.6	214	3.5	1.2
	1314	7	<1	–	7.6	214	3.5	0.5
	1316	8	<1	–	7.6	214	3.5	0.3
	1318	9	<1	–	7.6	214	3.6	0.1
	1320	11	<1	–	7.5	215	3.6	0.1
06-27-07	1100	0.6	<1	10.6	8.0	200	13.6	0.0
	1102	1	<1	10.5	8.2	200	13.5	0.0
	1104	2	<1	10.5	8.2	200	13.3	0.0
	1106	3	<1	10.4	8.3	200	13.3	0.5
	1108	4	<1	10.4	8.2	200	13.3	0.5
	1110	5	<1	11.0	8.2	201	11.7	1.0
	1112	6	<1	11.3	8.2	201	10.9	1.0
	1114	7	<1	11.4	8.2	201	7.0	1.0
	1116	8.1	<1	11.5	8.1	202	9.4	1.5
	1118	9.2	<1	11.7	8.1	203	7.8	1.5
	1120	10.1	<1	11.2	7.9	207	5.7	1.5
	1122	11	<1	10.9	7.9	208	5.3	2.3
				Chilchukabena Lake				
04-01-07	1156	0	<1	2.1	6.7	184	0.8	3.9
	1158	0.5	<1	1.6	6.7	180	2.0	2.6
	1200	1.5	<1	1.1	6.7	175	3.4	4.9
	1202	2.5	<1	0.6	6.7	175	3.3	–
08-28-07	1457	0.39	16	12.9	9.8	101	18.5	–
	1459	0.91	14	12.7	9.7	100	17.5	–
	1501	1.4	11	11.5	9.6	99	17.3	–
	1503	1.9	8.3	8.9	9.3	98	17.0	–
	1505	2.4	6	7.8	9.1	99	16.9	–
	1507	2.9	5.6	7.5	9.0	99	16.9	–

Table 8   25

Table 8. Field parameters for lake water-quality samples from Wonder Lake, Chilchukabena Lake, and Lake Minchumina, Denali National Park and Preserve and surrounding area, Alaska.—Continued

[Location of sampling sites are shown in figure 2. FNU, Formazin Nephelometric Unit; <, less then detection limit; m, meter; mg/L, milligram per liter; μS/cm, microsiemen per centimeter at 25 degrees Celsius; C, Celsius; –, missing value]

Date	Time	Depth sample (m) 00098	Turbidity, field YSI (FNU) 63680	Oxygen, dissolved (mg/L) 00300	pH, field 00400	Specific conductance, field (μS/cm) 00095	Water temperature (°C) 00020	Phyto-plankton, chlorophyll uncorrected (mg/L) 32234
				Lake Minchumina				
04-02-07	1210	0	1.0	–	7.6	259	0.2	5.7
	1212	0.5	1.0	–	7.6	257	0.4	5.5
	1214	1	1.0	–	7.5	254	0.6	4.8
	1216	1.5	1.0	–	7.5	252	0.8	4.9
	1218	2	1.0	–	7.4	251	0.9	5.4
	1220	3	1.0	–	7.4	249	1.3	5.3
	1222	4	1.0	–	7.4	247	1.6	5.6
	1224	5	1.0	–	7.3	246	2.0	5.6
	1226	6	1.0	–	7.3	249	2.5	4.8
	1228	7	1.0	–	7.1	260	3.0	5.2
	1230	8	1.5	–	7.0	281	3.6	5.6
	1232	8.3	1.0	–	6.9	307	4.0	6.0
08-28-07	1220	0.4	1.7	9.6	8.2	234	17.7	–
	1222	0.9	1.9	9.6	8.3	234	17.5	–
	1224	1.4	2.0	9.6	8.3	234	17.3	–
	1226	1.9	2.4	9.5	8.3	234	17.3	–
	1228	2.4	2.3	9.5	8.3	234	17.2	–
	1230	2.9	2.3	9.4	8.3	235	17.2	–
	1232	3.4	2.4	9.4	8.3	235	17.2	–
	1234	4.4	3.8	9.0	8.1	236	16.9	–
	1236	4.9	7.4	8.1	7.9	238	16.1	–
	1238	5.4	9.8	7.8	7.9	239	15.9	–
	1240	5.9	12.0	7.9	7.9	240	15.9	–
	1242	6.4	15.0	8.0	7.9	241	15.8	–
	1244	6.9	55.0	8.0	7.9	245	15.5	–
	1246	7.4	53.0	8.3	7.9	251	15.2	–
	1248	8.7	46.0	8.1	7.8	251	15.2	–

Table 9.   Concentrations of selected major ions, nutrients and trace elements in water samples from lake sampling sites, Denali National Park and Preserve and surrounding area, Alaska.

[Location of sampling sites are shown in figure 2. **Parameters**: Dis fet lab, Dissolved fixed end-point titration in laboratory; Dis tot IT Field, Dissolved total Incremental Titration in the field; Dis IT Field, Dissolved Incremental Titration in the field. FNU, Formazin Nephelometric Unit; Hg, mercury; CaCO$_3$, calcium carbonate; NO$_2$, nitrite; NO$_3$, nitrate; MF, membrane filter; E, estimated value. <, less than detection limit; m, meter; mm, millimeter; mL, milliliter; mg/L, milligram per liter; µS/cm, microsiemen per centimeter at 25 degrees Celsius; C, Celsius; col/100 mL, colonies per 100 milliliters; –, missing value]

Date	Time	Depth, sample (m) 00098	Depth, lake (m) 82903	Trans-parency, Secchi disk (m) 49701	Turbidity, field (FNU) 63680	Barometric pressure (mm of Hg) 00025	Oxygen, dissolved (mg/L) 00300	pH, field (units) 00400	pH, laboratory (units) 00403
Wonder Lake—site 1									
06-20-06	09:40	1.0	13.5	6.1	<1	709	10.3	8.2	8.2
06-20-06	09:50	11.0	13.5	–	<1	709	10.7	7.9	8.1
07-25-06	10:35	2.0	18.5	6.7	<1	699	9.7	8.3	8.3
07-25-06	10:40	15.0	18.5	–	<1	699	10.7	7.9	8.0
09-07-06	10:20	1.0	19.0	7.6	<1	703	10.7	8.3	8.3
09-07-06	10:30	1.0	19.0	7.6	<1	703	10.6	8.3	8.3
09-07-06	10:50	16.5	19.0	–	<1	702	10.5	7.8	8.0
Wonder Lake—site 2									
06-20-06	11:15	1.0	74.0	8.2	<1	709	10.4	8.1	–
06-20-06	11:30	55.0	74.0	–	<1	709	9.1	7.7	7.9
07-25-06	13:30	2.0	74.0	7.3	<1	699	9.5	8.3	8.2
07-25-06	14:10	64.0	74.0	–	<1	699	–	–	7.9
09-07-06	13:00	1.0	74.0	9.6	<1	703	10.4	8.4	8.3
09-07-06	13:30	45.0	74.0	–	<1	703	9.7	7.6	7.9
06-26-07	13:20	1.0	74.0	–	–	716	10.5	8.2	8.1
06-26-07	13:30	1.0	74.0	–	–	716	10.5	8.2	8.1
06-26-07	14:00	55.0	74.0	–	–	716	9.7	8.0	7.9
08-30-07	13:30	2.0	74.0	9.8	<1	705	9.6	8.4	8.3
08-30-07	14:00	55.0	74.0	–	<1	705	8.6	7.7	7.8
Wonder Lake—site 3									
06-20-06	12:40	1.0	20.5	7.0	<1	709	10.6	8.2	–
06-20-06	12:50	18.0	20.5	–	<1	709	10.2	8.0	8.0
07-25-06	16:10	2.0	24.2	7.6	<1	699	9.6	8.4	8.3
07-25-06	16:40	22.0	24.2	–	<1	699	10.3	7.7	7.9
09-07-06	15:05	1.0	20.0	8.7	<1	703	11.8	8.4	8.3
09-07-06	15:20	16.0	20.0	–	<1	703	11.1	7.8	7.9
04-01-07	14:30	2.0	11.0	–	<1	716	–	7.6	7.9
06-27-07	12:00	1.0	11.3	–	<1	715	10.3	7.8	8.2
06-27-07	12:15	9.0	11.3	–	<1	715	11.5	7.6	8.1
Chilchukabena Lake									
08-28-07	15:20	2.0	3.2	0.2	16.0	700	9.0	9.3	9.1
Lake Minchumina									
04-02-07	12:00	2.0	8.3	–	<1	753	12.3	7.4	7.7
08-28-07	13:15	2.0	9.3	0.6	9.6	699	8.9	8.2	8.2
08-28-07	13:25	2.0	9.3	0.6	9.7	700	8.7	8.3	8.2

Table 9   27

Table 9.   Concentrations of selected major ions, nutrients and trace elements in water samples from lake sampling sites, Denali National Park and Preserve and surrounding area, Alaska.—Continued

[Location of sampling sites are shown in figure 2. **Parameters**: Dis fet lab, Dissolved fixed end-point titration in laboratory; Dis tot IT Field, Dissolved total Incremental Titration in the field; Dis IT Field, Dissolved Incremental Titration in the field. FNU, Formazin Nephelometric Unit; Hg, mercury; CaCO$_3$, calcium carbonate; NO$_2$, nitrite; NO$_3$, nitrate; MF, membrane filter; E, estimated value. <, less than detection limit; m, meter; mm, millimeter; mL, milliliter; mg/L, milligram per liter; µS/cm, microsiemen per centimeter at 25 degrees Celsius; C, Celsius; col/100 mL, colonies per 100 milliliters; –, missing value]

Date	Time	Specific conductance, field (µS/cm) 00095	Specific conductance, laboratory (µS/cm) 90095	Air temperature (°C) 00020	Water temperature (°C) 00020	Calcium (mg/L) 00915	Magnesium (mg/L) 00925	Potassium (mg/L) 00935	Sodium (mg/L) 00930
				Wonder Lake—site 1					
06-20-06	09:40	197	196	–	12.4	32.3	4.41	0.78	1.10
06-20-06	09:50	204	201	–	6.2	32.7	4.38	0.79	1.09
07-25-06	10:35	196	196	–	16.0	31.0	4.32	0.77	1.07
07-25-06	10:40	206	205	–	5.4	33.5	4.49	0.78	1.11
09-07-06	10:20	194	200	–	11.5	31.9	4.19	0.76	1.13
09-07-06	10:30	194	200	–	11.5	32.0	4.18	0.77	1.13
09-07-06	10:50	206	212	–	5.4	34.2	4.38	0.81	1.18
				Wonder Lake—site 2					
06-20-06	11:15	–	–	–	11.5	–	–	–	–
06-20-06	11:30	212	211	–	3.8	34.6	4.70	0.81	1.16
07-25-06	13:30	196	195	–	16.2	32.6	4.18	0.80	1.14
07-25-06	14:10	–	210	–	–	33.8	4.57	0.80	1.11
09-07-06	13:00	194	200	–	11.5	31.2	4.16	0.73	1.09
09-07-06	13:30	211	216	–	4.0	34.9	4.52	0.85	1.19
06-26-07	13:20	199	205	–	13.2	32.9	4.25	0.73	1.17
06-26-07	13:30	198	205	–	13.2	33.4	4.31	0.78	1.23
06-26-07	14:00	206	218	–	4.0	34.6	4.45	0.80	1.23
08-30-07	13:30	197	198	15.0	14.6	32.5	4.46	0.78	1.10
08-30-07	14:00	213	215	15.0	4.2	35.3	4.78	0.83	1.17
				Wonder Lake—site 3					
06-20-06	12:40	196	–	–	11.2	–	–	–	
06-20-06	12:50	206	205	–	4.8	33.6	4.56	0.83	1.17
07-25-06	16:10	196	194	–	16.0	31.4	4.21	0.75	1.07
07-25-06	16:40	208	206	–	4.6	33.6	4.43	0.80	1.11
09-07-06	15:05	195	201	–	11.3	31.8	4.22	0.76	1.10
09-07-06	15:20	208	214	–	4.9	34.7	4.46	0.79	1.18
04-01-07	14:30	219	219	4.5	4.0	36.2	4.76	0.80	1.31
06-27-07	12:00	200	205	–	15.4	32.8	4.24	0.73	1.13
06-27-07	12:15	202	209	–	12.5	34.0	4.38	0.75	1.19
				Chilchukabena Lake					
08-28-07	15:20	98	100	–	15.6	11.9	3.97	0.62	2.94
				Lake Minchumina					
04-02-07	12:00	251	256	4.5	0.9	38.6	6.89	1.74	3.44
08-28-07	13:15	234	238	15.1	18.2	36.1	6.01	1.83	2.69
08-28-07	13:25	234	238	15.1	18.4	36.5	6.08	1.84	2.74

Table 9. Concentrations of selected major ions, nutrients and trace elements in water samples from lake sampling sites, Denali National Park and Preserve and surrounding area, Alaska.—Continued

[Location of sampling sites are shown in figure 2. **Parameters:** Dis fet lab, Dissolved fixed end-point titration in laboratory; Dis tot IT Field, Dissolved total Incremental Titration in the field; Dis IT Field, Dissolved Incremental Titration in the field. FNU, Formazin Nephelometric Unit; Hg, mercury; CaCO$_3$, calcium carbonate; NO$_2$, nitrite; NO$_3$, nitrate; MF, membrane filter; E, estimated value. <, less than detection limit; m, meter; mm, millimeter; mL, milliliter; mg/L, milligram per liter; μS/cm, microsiemen per centimeter at 25 degrees Celsius; C, Celsius; col/100 mL, colonies per 100 milliliters; –, missing value]

Date	Time	Alkalinity, Dis fet Lab, as CaCO$_3$ (mg/L) 39086	Alkalinity, Dis tot IT Field (mg/L) 29801	Bicarbonate, Dis IT Field (mg/L) 00453	Chloride (mg/L) 00940	Fluoride (mg/L) 00950	Silica (mg/L) 00955	Sulfate (mg/L) 00945	Solids, residue at 180°C, dissolved (mg/L) 70300
				Wonder Lake—site 1					
06-20-06	09:40	–	83	101	0.22	< 0.10	3.83	14	118
06-20-06	09:50	–	–	–	E 0.19	< 0.10	4.09	14.4	125
07-25-06	10:35	–	83	101	E 0.15	< 0.10	3.21	14.1	111
07-25-06	10:40	–	88	107	E 0.14	< 0.10	4.00	14.7	119
09-07-06	10:20	–	83	101	E 0.14	< 0.10	3.12	13.8	109
09-07-06	10:30	–	83	101	< 0.20	< 0.10	3.14	13.7	115
09-07-06	10:50	–	88	107	E 0.13	< 0.10	4.02	14.5	112
				Wonder Lake—site 2					
06-20-06	11:15	–	–	–	–	–	–	–	–
06-20-06	11:30	–	91	111	E 0.19	< 0.10	4.65	15.1	125
07-25-06	13:30	–	84	102	E 0.10	< 0.10	3.26	14.1	107
07-25-06	14:10	–	90	109	E 0.15	< 0.10	4.47	15.2	112
09-07-06	13:00	–	85	104	E 0.15	< 0.10	3.12	13.7	107
09-07-06	13:30	–	92	112	E 0.17	< 0.10	4.59	14.8	116
06-26-07	13:20	90	86	105	1.03	< 0.10	3.66	14.7	123
06-26-07	13:30	91	87	104	0.17	< 0.10	3.64	14.8	127
06-26-07	14:00	97	92	112	0.19	< 0.10	4.46	15.8	130
08-30-07	13:30	89	79	96	0.16	< 0.10	3.16	14.7	121
08-30-07	14:00	96	86	105	0.17	< 0.10	4.73	15.7	144
				Wonder Lake—site 3					
06-20-06	12:40	–	84	102	–	–	–	–	–
06-20-06	12:50	–	–	–	0.20	< 0.10	4.18	14.6	123
07-25-06	16:10	–	82	100	E 0.12	< 0.10	3.15	14.1	110
07-25-06	16:40	–	89	108	E 0.14	< 0.10	4.11	14.8	121
09-07-06	15:05	–	85	104	E 0.2	< 0.10	3.14	13.8	119
09-07-06	15:20	–	91	111	E 0.1	< 0.10	4.31	14.5	120
04-01-07	14:30	–	93	113	0.13	< 0.10	4.34	15.7	135
06-27-07	12:00	92	84	102	0.16	< 0.10	3.65	14.8	125
06-27-07	12:15	93	86	105	0.14	E 0.06	3.90	15.2	121
				Chilchukabena Lake					
08-28-07	15:20	50	44	54	0.32	0.60	4.11	0.25	72
				Lake Minchumina					
04-02-07	12:00	–	95	116	0.59	0.22	9.63	31	181
08-28-07	13:15	89	80	98	0.52	0.21	7.21	29.9	155
08-28-07	13:25	89	80	98	0.50	0.22	7.29	29.7	159

Table 9   29

Table 9. Concentrations of selected major ions, nutrients and trace elements in water samples from lake sampling sites, Denali National Park and Preserve and surrounding area, Alaska.—Continued

[Location of sampling sites are shown in figure 2. **Parameters**: Dis fet lab, Dissolved fixed end-point titration in laboratory; Dis tot IT Field, Dissolved total Incremental Titration in the field; Dis IT Field, Dissolved Incremental Titration in the field. FNU, Formazin Nephelometric Unit; Hg, mercury; CaCO$_3$, calcium carbonate; NO$_2$, nitrite; NO$_3$, nitrate; MF, membrane filter; E, estimated value. <, less than detection limit; m, meter; mm, millimeter; mL, milliliter; mg/L, milligram per liter; μS/cm, microsiemen per centimeter at 25 degrees Celsius; C, Celsius; col/100 mL, colonies per 100 milliliters; –, missing value]

Date	Time	Nitrogen, ammonia + organic, dissolved (mg/L) 00623	Nitrogen, ammonia + organic, total (mg/L) 00625	Nitrogen, ammonia, dissolved (mg/L) 00608	Nitrogen, NO$_2$+NO$_3$, dissolved (mg/L) 00631	Nitrogen, nitrite, dissolved (mg/L) 00613	Ortho-phosphorus (mg/L) 00671	Phosphorus (mg/L) 00666	Phosphorus, total (mg/L) 00665
| Wonder Lake—site 1										
06-20-06	09:40	0.20	E 0.10	E 0.008	0.033	< 0.002	< 0.006	< 0.004	< 0.004
06-20-06	09:50	0.17	E 0.09	< 0.010	0.048	< 0.002	E 0.004	< 0.004	E 0.002
07-25-06	10:35	E 0.09	0.15	E 0.007	< 0.016	< 0.002	< 0.006	E 0.004	0.004
07-25-06	10:40	E 0.09	0.11	< 0.010	0.330	< 0.002	< 0.006	< 0.004	0.004
09-07-06	10:20	0.27	0.12	E 0.005	< 0.016	< 0.002	< 0.006	< 0.007	E 0.004
09-07-06	10:30	0.27	0.13	E 0.005	< 0.016	< 0.002	< 0.006	< 0.004	0.004
09-07-06	10:50	0.20	E 0.10	E 0.005	0.035	< 0.002	< 0.006	< 0.004	0.014
| Wonder Lake—site 2										
06-20-06	11:15	–	–	–	–	–	–	–	–
06-20-06	11:30	0.22	E 0.08	< 0.010	0.087	E 0.001	< 0.006	< 0.004	E 0.003
07-25-06	13:30	0.14	0.13	E 0.005	< 0.016	< 0.002	< 0.006	< 0.004	0.005
07-25-06	14:10	0.13	E 0.09	< 0.010	0.085	E 0.001	< 0.006	< 0.004	0.004
09-07-06	13:00	0.29	0.13	E 0.008	< 0.016	< 0.002	< 0.006	< 0.004	E 0.003
09-07-06	13:30	0.22	0.12	E 0.007	0.093	0.003	< 0.006	< 0.004	E 0.003
06-26-07	13:20	0.12	0.14	< 0.020	0.021	< 0.002	< 0.006	< 0.006	< 0.008
06-26-07	13:30	0.19	0.27	< 0.020	0.021	< 0.002	0.011	< 0.006	< 0.008
06-26-07	14:00	E 0.09	0.14	< 0.020	0.069	< 0.002	< 0.006	< 0.006	< 0.008
08-30-07	13:30	0.22	E 0.08	< 0.020	< 0.016	< 0.002	< 0.006	< 0.006	< 0.008
08-30-07	14:00	0.12	< 0.10	< 0.020	0.085	< 0.002	< 0.006	< 0.006	< 0.008
| Wonder Lake—site 3										
06-20-06	12:40	0.17	E 0.07	< 0.010	0.040	< 0.002	E 0.004	E 0.002	0.130
06-20-06	12:50	0.25	0.12	< 0.010	0.056	< 0.002	< 0.006	< 0.004	E 0.002
07-25-06	16:10	0.18	0.12	< 0.010	< 0.016	< 0.002	< 0.006	< 0.004	E 0.003
07-25-06	16:40	E 0.09	0.13	< 0.010	0.051	< 0.002	< 0.006	< 0.004	0.005
09-07-06	15:05	0.22	0.14	< 0.010	< 0.016	< 0.002	< 0.006	< 0.004	< 0.004
09-07-06	15:20	0.26	0.12	E 0.008	0.058	< 0.002	< 0.006	< 0.004	E 0.002
04-01-07	14:30	0.39	0.39	< 0.020	0.160	< 0.002	0.012	0.018	0.025
06-27-07	12:00	0.12	0.14	< 0.020	0.022	< 0.002	< 0.006	< 0.006	< 0.008
06-27-07	12:15	0.13	0.26	< 0.020	0.025	< 0.002	< 0.006	< 0.006	< 0.008
| Chilchukabena Lake										
08-28-07	15:20	0.69	1.10	0.057	< 0.016	< 0.002	< 0.006	0.012	0.043
| Lake Minchumina										
04-02-07	12:00	E 0.08	E 0.08	< 0.020	0.740	< 0.002	< 0.006	< 0.006	< 0.008
08-28-07	13:15	0.33	0.23	< 0.020	< 0.016	< 0.002	< 0.006	E 0.004	0.014
08-28-07	13:25	0.29	0.26	< 0.020	< 0.016	E 0.002	E 0.003	E 0.004	0.014

Table 9. Concentrations of selected major ions, nutrients and trace elements in water samples from lake sampling sites, Denali National Park and Preserve and surrounding area, Alaska.—Continued

[Location of sampling sites are shown in figure 2. **Parameters:** Dis fet lab, Dissolved fixed end-point titration in laboratory; Dis tot IT Field, Dissolved total Incremental Titration in the field; Dis IT Field, Dissolved Incremental Titration in the field. FNU, Formazin Nephelometric Unit; Hg, mercury; CaCO₃, calcium carbonate; NO₂, nitrite; NO₃, nitrate; MF, membrane filter; E, estimated value. <, less than detection limit; m, meter; mm, millimeter; mL, milliliter; mg/L, milligram per liter; μS/cm, microsiemen per centimeter at 25 degrees Celsius; C, Celsius; col/100 mL, colonies per 100 milliliters; –, missing value]

Date	Time	Carbon, organic (mg/L) 00681	Entero-cocci, mEI MF (col/100 mL) 90909	*E coli*, m_TEC MF (col/100 mL) 31633	Phytoplankton, chlorophyll-*a* (mg/L) 70953	Phytoplankton, pheophytin-*a* (mg/L) 62360	Iron (mg/L) 01046	Manganese (mg/L) 01056
Wonder Lake—site 1
06-20-06	09:40	1.9	–	–	0.9	0.2	E 4	1.0
06-20-06	09:50	1.8	–	–	2.5	0.8	E 4	0.7
07-25-06	10:35	2.1	< 1	< 1	0.8	0.2	< 6	E 0.3
07-25-06	10:40	1.7	–	–	2.4	1.3	< 6	E 0.3
09-07-06	10:20	1.8	–	–	0.6	0.1	< 6	< 0.6
09-07-06	10:30	1.8	–	–	0.6	0.2	< 6	< 0.6
09-07-06	10:50	1.4	–	–	2.7	1.0	< 6	< 0.6
Wonder Lake—site 2
06-20-06	11:15	–	–	–	–	0.2	–	–
06-20-06	11:30	2.0	–	–	0.2	0.1	< 6	E 0.3
07-25-06	13:30	1.9	< 1	< 1	0.8	0.3	< 6	E 0.3
07-25-06	14:10	1.7	–	–	0.2	0.2	E 4	< 0.6
09-07-06	13:00	1.8	–	–	0.6	0.1	E 3	< 0.6
09-07-06	13:30	1.4	–	–	0.2	0.2	< 6	< 0.6
06-26-07	13:20	2.1	–	–	–	–	< 6	0.7
06-26-07	13:30	2.6	–	–	–	–	< 6	0.6
06-26-07	14:00	1.9	–	–	–	–	< 6	0.2
08-30-07	13:30	2.0	–	–	–	–	< 6	E 0.2
08-30-07	14:00	1.6	–	–	–	–	< 6	E 0.1
Wonder Lake—site 3
06-20-06	12:40	1.9	–	–	0.7	0.2	–	–
06-20-06	12:50	2.0	–	–	2.0	0.6	E 3	0.7
07-25-06	16:10	2.1	< 1	< 1	0.8	0.3	< 6	E 0.4
07-25-06	16:40	1.7	–	–	1.9	1.0	< 6	E 0.3
09-07-06	15:05	1.8	< 1	< 1	0.7	0.2	< 6	< 0.6
09-07-06	15:20	1.4	–	–	0.8	0.7	E 3	< 0.6
04-01-07	14:30	12.6	–	–	–	–	< 6	< 0.2
06-27-07	12:00	2.1	–	–	–	–	< 6	0.7
06-27-07	12:15	2.2	–	–	–	–	< 6	0.4
Chilchukabena Lake
08-28-07	15:20	7.7	–	–	–	–	78	6.8
Lake Minchumina
04-02-07	12:00	1.6	–	–	–	–	275	20.7
08-28-07	13:15	7.5	–	–	–	–	11	0.7
08-28-07	13:25	7.5	–	–	–	–	10	0.6